# The Last of Us Part I Complete Guide

Jimmi Laustsen

ISBN: 979-8-8496-8470-3

# CONTENTS

Warehouse Key*

The Last of Us 1 is a survival horror game created by PlayStation Studios developer Naughty Dog which first released in 2013. This The Last of Us 1 walkthrough, which includes all collectibles, is based on The Last of Us: Part I for PS5 and PC, which is also known as The Last of Us Remake. However, its content also applies to The Last of Us Remastered (PS4) and The Last of Us (PS3), unless explicitly stated otherwise. For reference, we awarded the title a 8/10 in our The Last of Us: Part I PS5 review, describing it as "a better, more beautiful remake of a modern classic".

This The Last of Us Part 1 guide contains everything you need, providing a complete walkthrough to the game. From safe codes to Tools, special weapons, supplements, collectibles and all the rest. We've got help for everything you're going to need in the the game, complete with pictures and pointers to make sure you don't miss anything that might help you endure and survive. It's a tough world out there so don't make it any harder than it needs to be.

## HOMETOWN

Beginning on what appears to be a normal evening, The Last of Us' Prologue chapter soon devolves into something far more sinister. This section will introduce you to the game's main protagonist and the core conflict they will face throughout the remainder of the game.

The Last of Us opens on a long cutscene introducing us to Sarah and her father, Joel. Once the scene ends, we'll cut back to Sarah, who is woken up by a late-night phone call.

Once the conversation concludes, Sarah will get out of bed and we'll take control. Our objective now is to go and find Joel. His bedroom is at the end of the corridor outside Sarah's room, but there are a few things for us to interact with before we get there.

Check out the dresser opposite Sarah's bed and you'll find a birthday card with a dinosaur on it. You can open the card by hitting **TRIANGLE**.

When you're ready, head through the door and follow the route ahead. Instead of taking a right at the end of the corridor, go through the doorway ahead of you. You'll find yourself in the bathroom. Have a read of the newspaper by the sink for a little hint of what's to come.

When you're ready, leave the bathroom and head for the doorway to the right of the staircase. Sarah will enter to find the room empty. After a few seconds of watching the nearby TV, you'll hear an explosion outside. That's our cue to leave. Head out the door and descend the staircase.

Once you reach the ground floor, you'll hear a phone going off in the kitchen. Head over to the kitchen drawers opposite the oven and you'll find Joel's phone. Interact with it and then head through the set of double doors on your left.

As you enter, Joel will run into the room and begin rummaging through a nearby desk, eventually pulling out a revolver. You'll then cue a cutscene, eventually culminating in Joel taking Sarah out to the front of the house where his brother, Tommy, is waiting in a car.

## Heading To The City

The next section will take place in Tommy's car. This isn't a cutscene and you're able to move freely, so take a look around as Tommy drives. There's a lot of harrowing stuff happening here, so you'll have a lot to look at.

The end of the scene sees Tommy, Joel and Sarah arrive in the city. After a brutal sequence of events, they'll find themselves in a crash, with Tommy's car flipped upside down.

Once the cutscene ends, you'll regain control, this time as Joel. When prompted, repeatedly hit SQUARE to kick the windscreen in and free yourself. After a short exchange, you'll hand your gun to Tommy and pick Sarah up. Follow the crowd through the streets ahead.

There's a lot going on here and no real danger just yet, so feel free to take a look at the chaos unfurling around you. As you reach the end of the street, an explosion will go off in front of the theatre ahead, causing Tommy to direct you down a nearby alleyway.

If you missed it, it's on the left-hand side of the street, just next to Anne's Flower Shop.

Follow him and run up the path ahead. You'll be attacked by an infected pedestrian. Mash SQUARE to knock him away, allowing Tommy to finish him off. Now, continue following the path. Eventually, infected will begin to jump over the walls and rush you. Stick to the path and follow Tommy.

He'll eventually lead you through the backdoor of a bar. Once inside, a cutscene will play. After it's finished and you've regained control, leave the bar and head through the crack in the brick wall ahead of you. It's marked by a spotlight and yellow hazard tape. Follow the route ahead. Infected will chase you, quickly catching up, but don't worry about avoiding them; this is intentional for the next story beat.

# QUARANTINE ZONE

**20 Years Later Walkthrough**

Optional Conversation #1

Shortly after the area with the civilians on their knees, opposite the checkpoint is a newspaper vending machine with a couple standing near to it. Get up close and they'll acknowledge Joel. Interact with them for an Optional Conversation.

After the Optional Conversation, head back to Tess and hand the guards at the checkpoint your papers. A truck will be bombed and you'll be locked in.

Sprint back the way you've just come, following Tess into a building on the left. She'll hand you a Health Kit, which you can equip by pushing up on the d-pad and use with the R2 button.

Follow Tess down the corridor to learn about a character named Marlene. Eventually you'll get to a large room with an entertainment centre on the left. Help Tess move it by holding down triangle and pushing right on the analogue stick. Then sneak through the hole to Beyond the Wall.

### Beyond the Wall Walkthrough

*Weapon: 9mm Pistol*

Directly ahead, as directed by Tess, you'll find your gear on a Workbench, which includes a 9mm Pistol, a torch, and a gas mask.

Meet back up with Tess, and push the triangle button to boost her up on the ledge. Then press triangle again to get her to pull you up. In this dark area, use the triangle button to push up the wooden barrier, and climb into the café.

---

### *Optional Conversation #1*

Immediately outside the café, through the front doorway, you'll get an Optional Conversation with Tess. Push the triangle button to start the discussion.

---

Follow Tess forward up the grassy hill and into a backyard type area. She'll mention that she's looking for a ladder, and you can find it behind the overgrown car directly ahead. Pick it up with triangle and then carry it back to the building on the right. Use it to climb up and through the hole in the wall. You'll come out in a room with a pool table.

Be sure to explore the kitchen tabletop immediately on the right of the next room, as this has Weapons Parts you can use to upgrade your weapons.

---

### Firefly Pendant #1: Vigil's Firefly Pendant

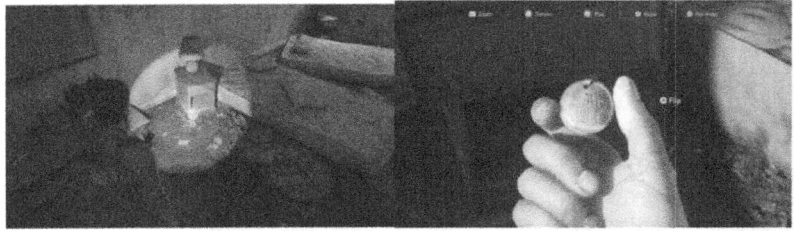

Before following Tess down the stairs, head into the bedroom directly across from the room you entered, and look in front of the small table next to the two mattresses on the ground. A Firefly Pendant named Vigil's Firefly Pendant is on the floor. Collecting this will unlock the Fallen Firefly Trophy.

---

Follow Tess down the stairs, and eventually she'll point out some spores in the next room. Wait for Joel to put on his gas mask, then on the right pay attention to the hole in the wall.

*Optional Conversation #2*

Crawl through the hole in the wall in the spores area by using the circle button. You can examine a dead corpse along the way to learn of the origins of the spores, which is an Optional Conversation opportunity.

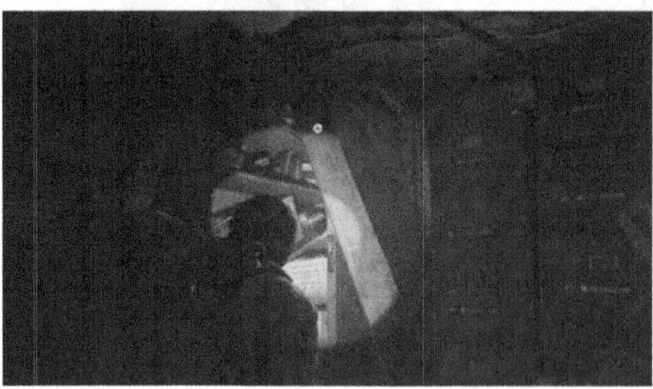

At the end of the corridor is a wooden beam blocking the way. Move it with triangle and then squeeze through the gap. A fellow survivor will plead with you to help them, and you can choose to either ignore their request or shoot them. Just remember to pick up the ammo on the floor.

Crouch under the blocked door and you'll instantly encounter some Clickers. The first enemy will be a tutorial, so hold R1 to activate Listen mode and then creep up behind them and execute a stealth kill. You can choose to sneak past the next two Clickers or kill them; if you're trying to conserve ammo, we'd recommend just crawling past.

In the kitchen, you can grab a Granola Bar from the counter, and there's a back room with a closed door that you can open with some ammo inside. Once you're done, head up some stairs to the Natale & Vegiard Legal Group.

---

**Artefact #1: Boston Q.Z. Map**

At this point you should be able to open your backpack by pushing the touchpad. You'll note that you already have a couple of Artefacts collected, the first is the Boston Q.Z. Map.

*Artefact #2: Military Pamphlet*

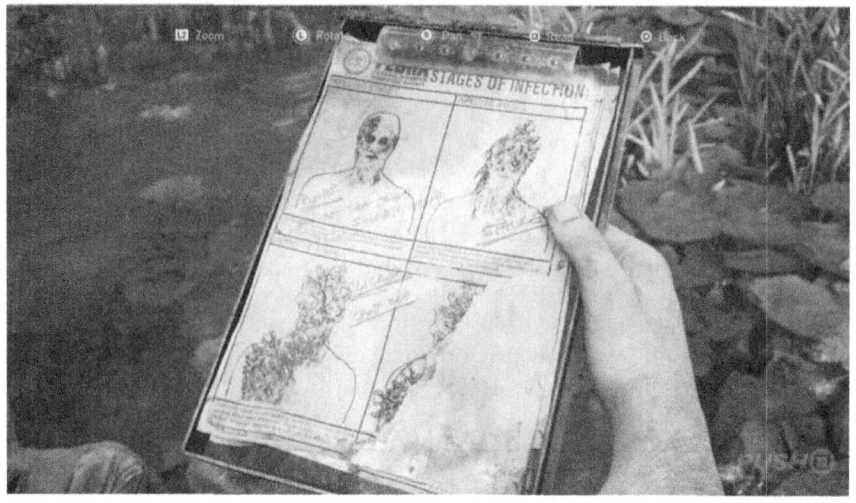

The second Artefact already in Joel's backpack is the Military Pamphlet.

*Artefact #3: Note to Brother*

Open the door on the left wall of the Natale & Vegiard Legal Group, and on the desk to the left is an Artefact named Note to Brother.

Now exit the building and drop down into the basketball court, following Tess through the swamp-like pond area and between some burned out buses.

Follow Tess towards the building, where she'll remove a wooden panel as a way to get in. Climb up and she'll note that the plank of wood that's used as a makeshift bridge has dropped into the room below. Follow the path around the room down to collect it.

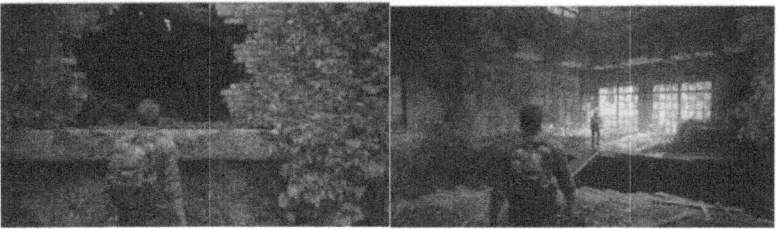

Pick up the plank with triangle and pass it to Tess who will take it off you. Then use the hole in the wall to climb back up to where Tess was, and cross the plank, using the left analogue stick to balance your body.

Follow Tess outside, down the stairs, and then around the alleyways until she unlocks a door.

### *Firefly Pendant #2: Glueck's Firefly Pendant*

Directly opposite the door Tess opens is a tree, and if you look closely at its rear branches you'll see a Firefly Pendant hanging in it. Shoot it down and pick it up to get Glueck's Firefly Pendant.

Head through the door Tess opened to continue onwards to The Slums, ensuring to collect some ammunition from the counter before exiting the room on the child's clearance.

## The Slums Walkthrough

Immediately at the beginning of this chapter, after you've been given the all-clear by the boy Tess pays, walk through the market-like area. This follows directly from Beyond the Wall. The people here are shady, so be sure to keep yourself to yourself. You'll eventually get on a bus, which is being used as a kind of makeshift shelter.

### *Artefact #1: Drafting Notice*

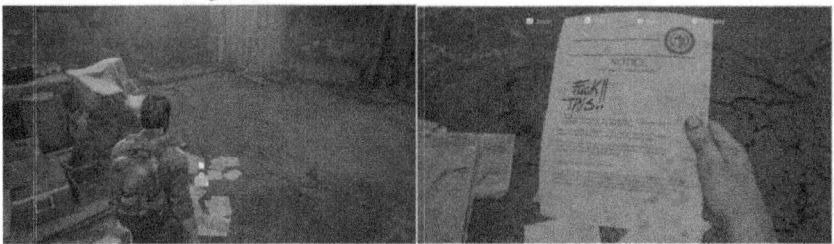

Once you get off the bus, head straight forwards and look for a puddle on the ground and a bunch of scattered papers. Pick up one page for an Artefact named Drafting Notice

Artefact #2: Wanted Poster

Move forward from where you found the previous Artefact and interact with the pinboard directly ahead. You'll get Wanted Poster, which reveals a little more about Marlene.

---

Once you've picked up the Artefacts, follow Tess down the alleyway, where she'll bribe a local thug. Get ready because you're about to be ambushed, so reload your weapon in preparation.

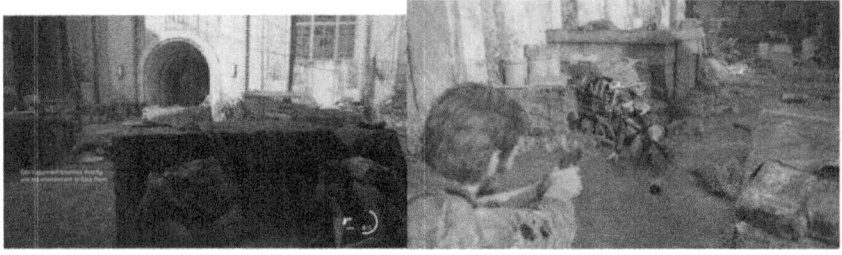

Tess will tell you to flank the thugs you fight in this courtyard area, so use the crates and boxes as cover to get the angle on them, and then use headshots to minimise the ammo you use. Once they're dead, follow Tess forward into another alleyway.

You'll need to boost Tess up onto the wall with triangle, and she'll in turn grab your arm and pull you up. Keep pushing forward until you reach a wire fence with a hole in it, and crawl through the gap.

As soon as you enter the courtyard, two guards will walk out of the building. You're going to take one each, so go for the goon on the right side and remain crouched to approach. Get a stealth kill, and then head back to the building they came from. There are two more baddies in here, and you can use Listen mode with R1 to pinpoint their precise location. Stealth kill the one closest to you and loot the body for the Warehouse Key, which is required to progress.

*Artefact #3: Warehouse Key\**

The Warehouse Key you loot to progress the story is listed as an Artefact in The Last of Us and The Last of Us Remastered, but not in The Last of Us: Part I. Either way, it's mandatory to continue the story.

---

In the next area, pick up the bottle from atop the crates and use it to lure the nearby enemies into a position where you can easily take them out. You can choose to use stealth or your guns here, but obviously it's always best to conserve as much ammo as possible. Head into the warehouse either up the staircase or through the front, but beware, there are some foes on the upper balcony which can be difficult to take out if you enter on the ground floor.

Once you've dealt with everyone, explore the offices on the upper-level of the warehouse for a Shiv and some Health.

Head back down to the ground floor of the warehouse, and use the metal rope chain to open the big sheet metal door. You'll automatically drop down into a shipyard area, which is one of the most challenging combat encounters in the game thus far.

There are a number of goons patrolling the outside of the docks that you'll want to deal with first. We recommend heading left and dealing with the guards on the left-side of the building, before using your bottles to disturb the patterns of the enemies inside the main building. Once you do go inside, be careful you don't get flanked, as goons will come from all sides — and potentially even behind you.

Once you've dealt with them all, there's a locked door right at the end of the building marked with a Dock 2 sign, but don't go through that just yet.

---

### Artefact #4: Shipping Manifest

In the docks area, where you first drop in, look to the rails on the right overlooking the ship graveyard. An Artefact named Shipping Manifest is on the floor.

*Artefact #5: Docks Notes*

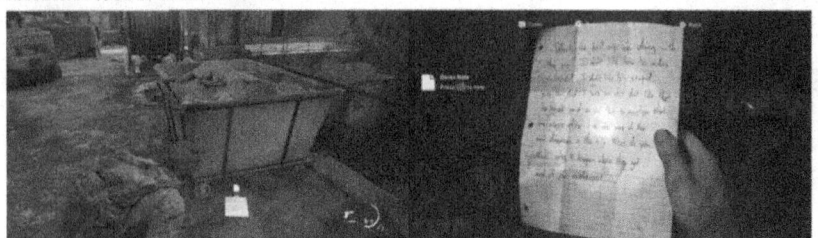

From the previous position, head inside the building, through its right entry point. You'll see two blue dumpsters with cloth and materials inside on the right. An Artefact named Docks Notes is just on the ground behind them.

---

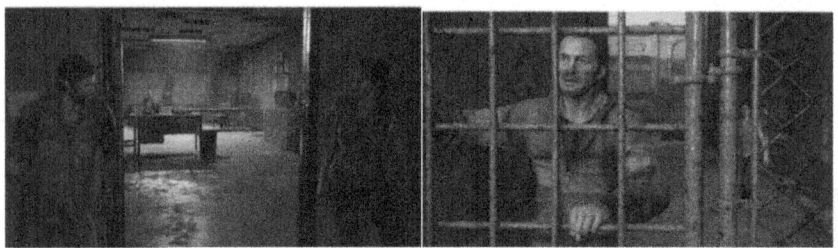

Once you've scavenged everything, head through the door mentioned above and you'll get into a chase with Robert. You need to keep up with him otherwise this will be a Game Over. Once you've caught up with him, watch the cutscene, and continue on with The Cargo.

**The Cargo Walkthrough**

Once the cutscene has concluded following The Slums, you're going to need to follow Marlene. Stick close behind her, and while there's no imminent danger, there's not a lot to look around at here.

Marlene will eventually lead you to a ladder you need to climb, which takes you to a metal staircase you can use to reach some roofing. Just keep following her lead — you can't really go wrong here.

nce you reach the rooftop, you'll witness an explosion off on the horizon, and Marlene will give some context about what's been going on. Follow her in through the window, and be sure to collect all the supplies on the table immediately in front of you. Then help her to open the door by pushing triangle and moving the analogue stick to the right.

Keep following Marlene down some stairs into a large opening. She'll point out that the doorway you need to reach is on the other side, but unfortunately it's swarming with guards. Crouch down and follow her up the staircase.

You're going to want to sneak into the building on the left at the top of the stairs, and stealth kill the guards if you can. Fortunately, Marlene will help you out. Sneak through the building, collecting any supplies along the way, and then head through the window and outside. Remember to use stealth kills if you possibly can; bricks and bottles can help you to pull the guards into different positions, granting you an opportunity to get the jump.

Once the coast is clear, you'll notice that Marlene has moved over to three corpses on the bridge.

*Optional Conversation #1*

Speak to Marlene while she's looking at the bodies on the bridge for an Optional Conversation.

---

Follow Marlene to the stairs, where it says Waterline St Number 33 on the large sign. Go down the stairs and reach the door that was mentioned earlier.

Now it's mostly a case of following Marlene through the building until you're introduced to an important character.

Marlene will explain in a cutscene that she wants you to help smuggle Ellie to a group of Fireflies at the Capitol Building. And, no, you're not in a position to argue really. When the cutscene concludes, you'll be out on an open street.

---

### Firefly Pendant #1: Liu's Firefly Pendant

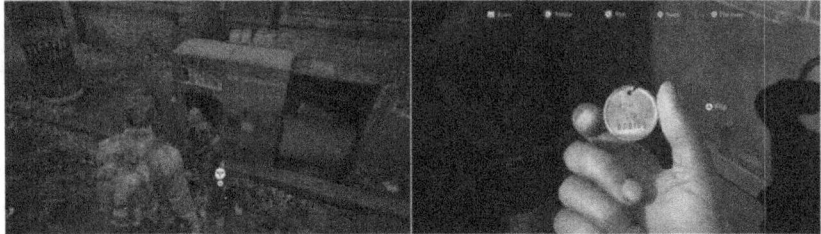

Directly opposite from the building where you met Ellie, there are a trio of newspaper vending machines. One has a corpse perched against it. Search next to the body for a Firefly Pendant named Liu's Firefly Pendant.

---

Follow the staircase down into a blocked off area, and use the staircase into a tunnel on the right to make your way around.

You'll eventually end up in an area where there's a staircase you can't reach. Run past it towards the garage beyond it, and grab the dumpster with triangle. Now wheel it backwards the staircase and vault on top of it to reach the staircase.

There's only one path you can take in this building, so just follow it around and enjoy the banter between Joel and Ellie. You'll eventually reach a door, so head inside and watch the cutscene, as you progress towards Outside.

# THE OUTSKIRTS

### Outside

Artifact 9: Tess' List

After talking to Tess, go back into the room that Joel was sleeping in. On the table by the couch, you can find it.

Now follow Tess through the hole in the wall behind the bookshelf.

Power up the generator by pressing Triangle at the right time, then take the lift down.

Artifact 10: Patrol Routes Map

Once you go down, you will find this to the right on the ground.

Go through the glowing-red hole in the wall.

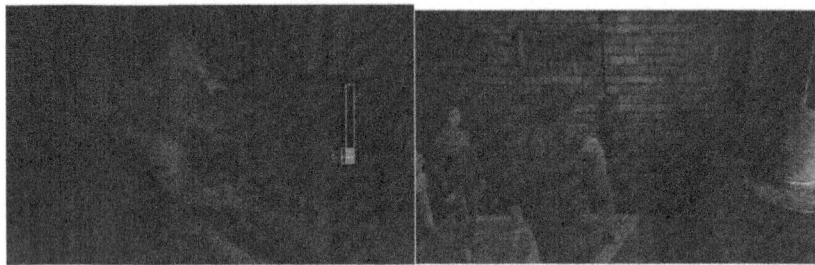

Continue forward up the ladder, then sneak outside. Advance forward into the truck with the lobster on it. Go through the truck and get ambushed. Well, LOTS of interesting things happen in this cutscene.

After all the excitement of that cutscene ends, crouch under the tanker to go forward.

Sneaky time! Follow Tess and avoid the spotlights.

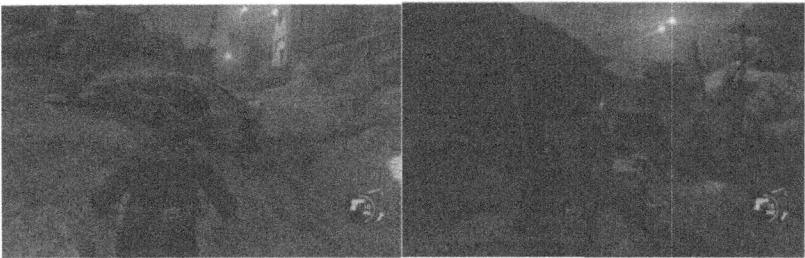

You get to a section where you have to run into a sewer drain, so follow Tess right in. From the sewer pipe, keep going to find a few more soldiers looking for you. Go off to the left to hide behind a building, then wrap yourself around the far side of the building.

Avoid the man up on the road here, and duck into another sewer pipe. Keep going forward until you can drop down into some water. From here, instead of going up the rubble hill straight ahead, go to your right and climb up the ledge here and to your right will be some scrap blades. Now go through the doorway ad up the rubble hill.

More guards show up who will shoot at you, so duck behind the wall to the left of the guard. Sneak forward into the house and head upstairs. Drop down from here into the next building. Go forward to find a big garage door that you can yank open. Before opening go through the window on the right and collect the supplies in the desk.

More stealth time! Go from behind the cop car to the tank to the building. Once in the building, hide as far as you can away to the right, then throw a brick back by the police car to distract the guards.

Move forward now, still aware of where the guards are, through the next building, through a truck, and eventually you drop down into a big hole in the middle of the street. Crawl through a sewer pipe down here right next to a makeshift flag.

You end up in a basement. Go up the stairs to find another small hole in the wall to crawl through. You hear that the guards are leaving so stay hidden for a few seconds as they clear out. Now cross the room. There is a big open doorway on the other side of the room, so go in here to grab supplies. Some may be hidden in the lockers in the room, so don't forget to check there as well.

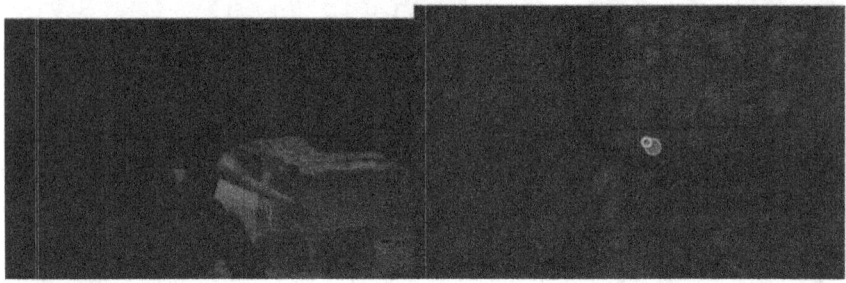

Now go back out the doorway and across the hall to another open pathway. Make your way through the pipe and the waist-deep water, then pop out through the gate on the other side of the room.

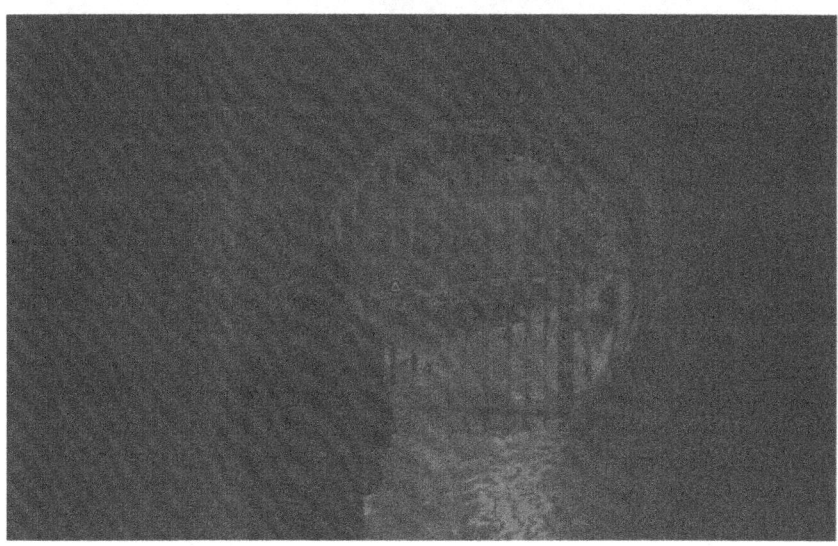

**Downtown**

Time to head back Outside into the rain, and this time we're heading downtown. Follow Tess, but when she goes up to the bridge, crouch underneath the gap and look for some Supplements on the left. Then make your way back the way Tess came, and up onto the bridge again.

---

Artefact #1: Evacuation Leaflet

As you make your way up the bridge and onto a street, look on the right for a traffic light. Directly beneath it you'll find the Artefact, which is named Evacuation Leaflet.

---

Follow the street forwards. Along the way you'll hear an ominous scream off into the distance, but don't let it deter you. Before you clamber up the soggy hill, head inside the 18-wheeler on your left and grab the Weapon Parts inside. Then go up the aforementioned hill and look over the edge. There's no way down so you're going to have to go around. Take the only path available to you around to The Goldstone Building.

---

Firefly Pendant #1: Lenz's Firefly Pendant

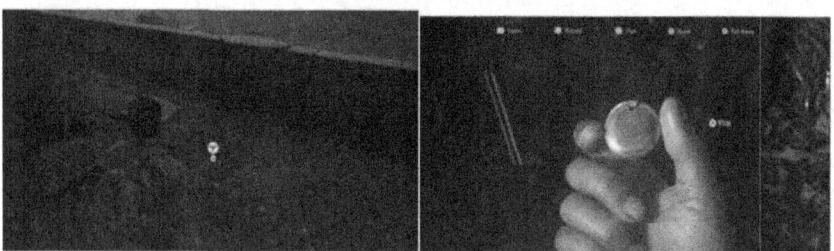

Before you head inside The Goldstone Building, just look at the trees directly after the building's sign. There's a Firefly Pendant named Lenz's Firefly Pendant hanging from a branch. Use a nearby brick to conserve ammo and toss it at the pendant to knock it down. Then pick it up.

---

Finally, you can go inside. There's a closed door on the left, which you can open and head inside for some resources. Once you're done, take the open door on the right.

Optional Conversation #1

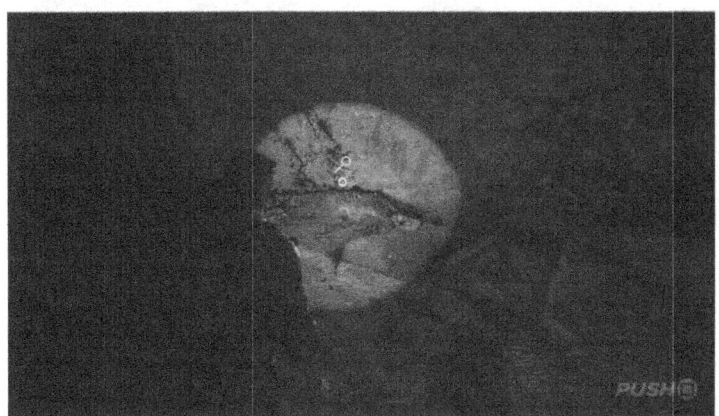

As you come in through this door, there's a dead body on the floor immediately on the other side of the doorway. Interact with it for an Optional Conversation.

Directly opposite the doorway you've just come through is another door you can open. Head inside the room to grab some weapon supplies from the long table ahead. Then go up the stairs.

Artefact #2: Field Ops Log

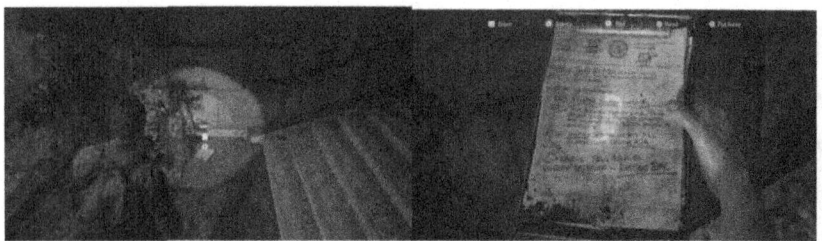

As you go up the stairs, you'll happen across another corpse slumped against the wall. Next to him is an Artefact named Field Ops Log.

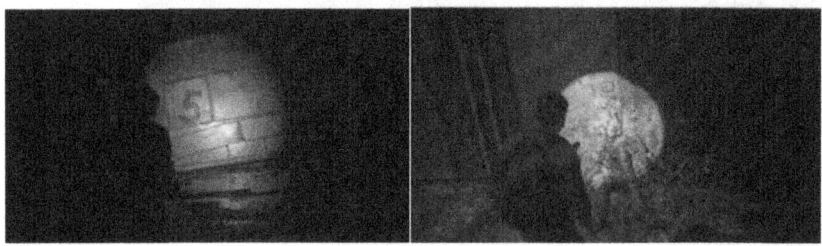

Keep going up the stairs. If you carry on to Level 6 at the top, you'll be able to get some additional supplies on the lower difficulty levels. Otherwise, get off at Level 5 and interact with the Clicker. Move it away from the doorway and then bust through into the next room.

Forge forward, remembering to collect supplies along the way. You'll end up in an area with office cubicles. Open the door to the right and you'll be ambushed by a Clicker. Tap the square button to escape its clutches.

Shiv Door #1

Immediately after you are confronted by the Clicker, head into the room on the right, and through the doorway. Directly opposite is a locked Shiv Door, so open it and loot the items inside.

---

Go back to the corridor where you were previously confronted by the Clicker, and take the exit on the left at the far end of the corridor. Boost Tess up and wait for her to haul you and Ellie over the edge. Then you'll find yourself in another room with another Clicker. This time use the bottles scattered across the floor to distract its attention, and make your way around the perimeter of the room to some scaffolding, which you can climb to escape.

Hop over the staircase, and then pull the drawers towards you to create an opening. Climb over and head outside of the building onto the window washing carts. Then make your way around the perimeter of the building and back inside, through an open doorway.

---

Weapon: Revolver

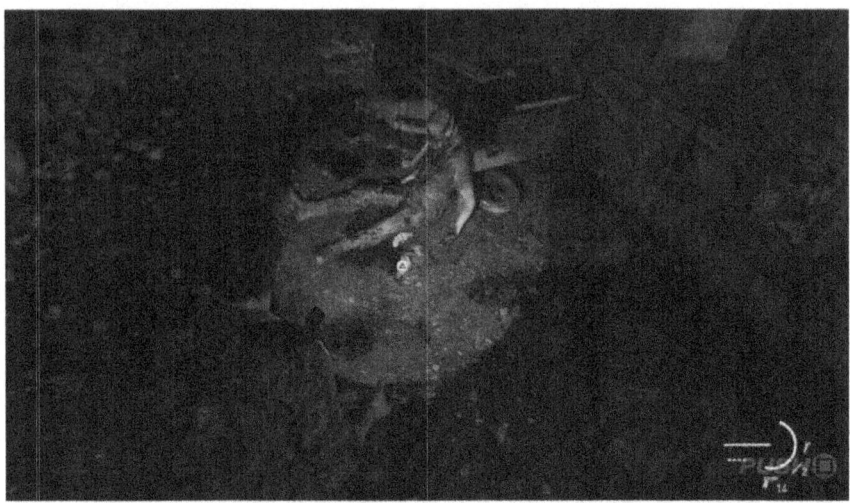

Immediately on the other side of the door is a corpse with a new Weapon named the Revolver.

---

Drop down the hole and immediately crouch. There are a ton of Runners and Clickers in this area, but if you approach carefully you can stealth kill them all. Take the first Runner immediately in front of you, and then the second on the left. Use a Shiv to kill the Clicker, and finally take the remaining two Runner in the end room. Once you're done, Joel will signal to Ellie and Tess that they can follow him down now.

Take the ramp up in the end room and interact with the big metal drawers. Drag them out of the way so that Tess and Ellie can make it into the next room, and they'll help you get a way through. You're now going to want to get left and down; basically follow the route until you reach a big sign that says Oliver on it. Remember to loot any supplies you discover along the way.

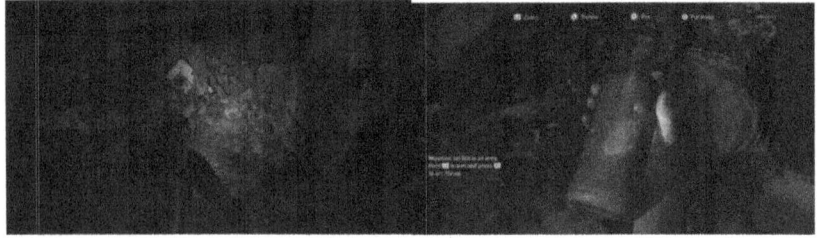

Keep working your way down until you end up in the subway. Directly ahead of you is a corpse with a discarded Molotov cocktail, which you're naturally going to want to grab.

---

Artefact #3: Firefly Map

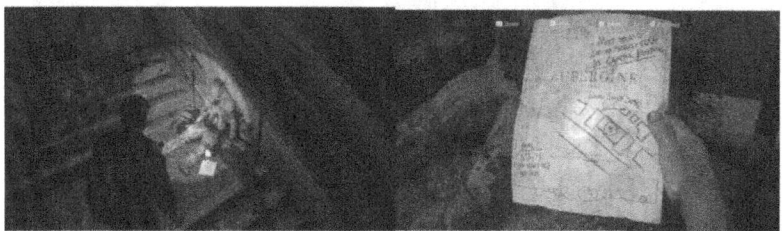

Directly ahead of where you found the Molotov are some stairs. Climb them to find a corpse, with an Artefact named Firefly Map next to it.

---

Make your way round the corner and into the room with all the Clickers. Remember you can use bricks and bottles to divert their attention, and also Shivs for an instant kill. Head to left first of all, and dispatch of the Runner outside the store. Then go behind the counter and open the drawer.

---

Artefact #4: Note to Derek

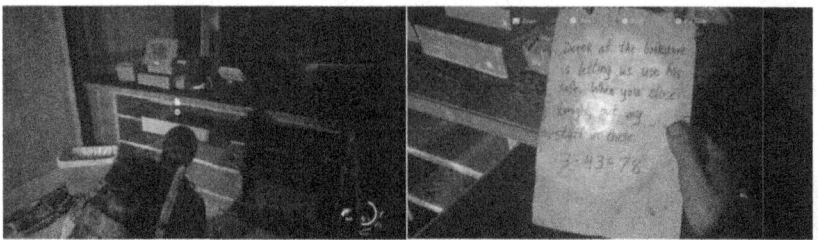

In the area with all the Clickers, shortly after the subway, on the left is a medicine shop. Inside the drawer of the medicine shop, you'll find some ammunition and an Artefact named Note to Derek.

Safe #1

On the opposite side of where you found Note to Derek, there's another shop named Round Note. There's a Runner in here, so just be careful to dispatch it. Once you're done, access the Safe with the combination code 03-43-78. You can find more information on how to open the Safe in Downtown through the link.

Go through the waiting room and back to the subway on the other side. Kill the Clicker waiting for you

**Museum**

In the aftermath of Downtown, head inside the open building and deal with the Runners inside. You should be able to stealth kill all three of these, so put your gun away and conserve ammo. Once you're done, grab the drawers and wheel it down to the truck trailer blocking the way ahead of you.

Artefact #1: Medical Pamphlet

After you climb over the seafood truck trailer, turn immediately back and climb inside.

At the rear, next to a wooden beam, is an Artefact named Medical Pamphlet.

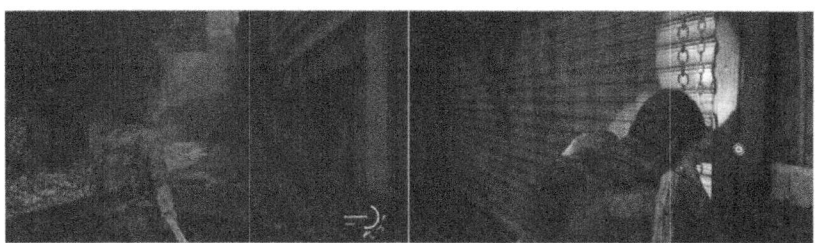

Keep walking forwards up the alleyway ahead of you, and open the metal garage door to the left. You might want to hurry, because you're about to get chased down.

Workbench #1

Immediately after shutting the garage door and escaping all the Runners, head left of the truck in the garage area before finding an exit. The Workbench is on the upper-level.

Before you leave the garage, look in the back of the truck trailer for some Supplements. Then head to the door just to the right of the Workbench. Loot the room with painting for supplies, and then go through the doors into the big room with the ramp in the middle. Head up.

Firefly Pendant #1: Kiper's Firefly Pendant

As you go up the ramp in the room with all the art and statues, climb up the left side and shimmy to the smashed display case. Inside is a Firefly Pendant called Kiper's Firefly Pendant.

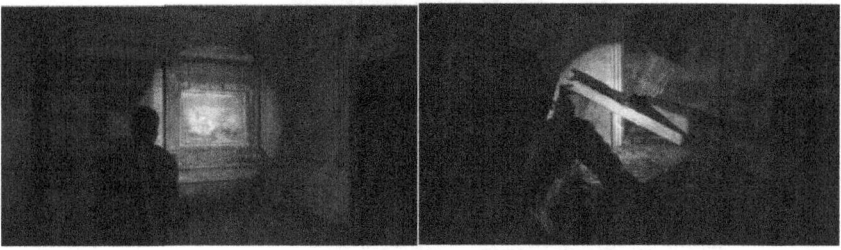

Now explore the museum, ensuring to search for any supplies along the way. Remember, it's always best to craft during quiet moments, so you have enough resources when the action increases, so take a bit of time to make some items. Eventually you'll reach a beam which you can lift up to let Tess and Ellie through, but it's going to break before you make it.

Turn back around and take the only pathway out. There are three Clickers in the museum with you, so use Listen mode to pinpoint their position and use your Shivs to stealth kill them. The area's quite large so you can go loud if you want to, but it's best to preserve your ammo in our opinion.

Shiv Door #1

After dealing with the Clickers in the museum, head inside the canteen area and look for a metal door on the right-hand side. It's a Shiv Door, so be sure to open it and loot the resources inside, including the Supplements and Weapon Parts.

---

Head to the end of the hallway and take the door after the canteen. Go up the stairs and sneak up on the Runner banging against the door. Stealth kill him to conserve your ammo. Once you go through the door, you're going to have to deal with more Runners, so prepare yourself. There are at least six of them, so prepare to go loud and make sure you have some Health Kits crafted.

---

Optional Conversation #1

After the big fight with all the Runners in the upstairs part of the museum, Tess and Ellie will walk over to an open window. Speak to Tess first for an Optional Conversation.

Optional Conversation #2

Immediately after Tess has finished talking, speaking to Ellie for another Optional Conversation.

---

Climb through the open window and then head up the stairs to the top of the building. You'll see The Capitol Building on the horizon. Grab the plank of wood, and use it to make a bridge.

## The Capitol Building

After descending from the Museum rooftops, it's time to make your way to your final destination: The Capitol Building. You can see it clearly on the horizon, so getting there shouldn't be a problem, should it? Follow Tess and Ellie down the stairs.

---

### Artefact #1: Firefly Orders

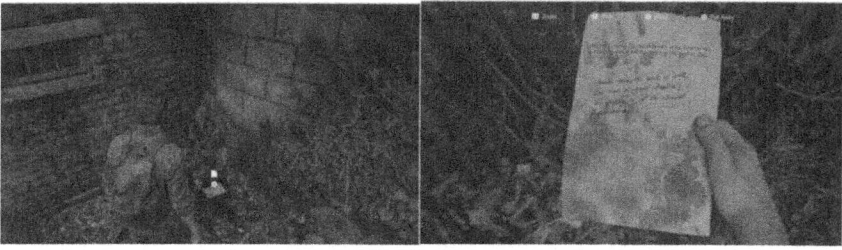

Take a right immediately at the bottom of the stairs at the start of the chapter, and find an Artefact next to the corpse named Firefly Orders. There's also some ammunition.

---

Grab the dumpster and push it towards the gate with the yellow construction tape above it. Climb up and over the scaffolding and head left, towards the Capitol Building and the gazebo on the horizon.

Firefly Pendant #1: Davidson's Firefly Pendant

Wade through the water up to the gazebo on the left, opposite the Capitol Building. In the middle, under the water, is a Firefly Pendant named Davidson's Firefly Pendant.

---

Forge forward into the Capitol Building, and strap yourself in for a pretty major cutscene. You may need a few seconds to catch your breath, but once you regain control, scoop up the supplies and head up the stairs on the right. Maybe don't look down to the foyer.

Head to the right into the next room and grab the Supplements from the corner of the podium. Then jump across to the next room, ensuring to stay ahead of the guards who are on your tail.

Weapon: Hunting Rifle

After you jump down into the third room in the Capitol Building, it's practically impossible to miss, but be sure to pick up a new Weapon, the Hunting Rifle, from the corpse perched between the conjoined doorways.

---

You're going to have an opportunity to test out that Hunting Rifle almost immediately, because at the opposite end of the room a bunch of enemies are going to funnel in. Use the side rooms to flank them, and remember you can swap between handguns and long guns quickly with the R1 button. Explore the side rooms for more supplies, including some Supplements on a desk. Once you're all done, head through the doorway at the end of the hallway where the troops came from, and go down the stairs.

Before you fall down, now is a good opportunity to reload your weapons and prepare. Drop from the stairs into the large open area and get ready to initiate combat. Use the side rooms and cover to get flanking opportunities. Then head back outside, into the water, and make your way towards the subway station opposite the Capitol Building.

You'll be blocked in by a convoy, so just sprint deep into the subway station until you reach an area with spores. A cutscene will trigger while you put on your mask. More guards will show up, so be sure to take them out using stealth kills, then grab the Supplements to the right of where you entered, perched atop the abandoned train cars.

Climb aboard the train filled with water on the far side of the tracks, and dive into the deep water. You can dive with circle and surface with the X button. Dive under the water and swim through a couple of passageways, continuing to move forwards in the same direction. Ellie will eventually find a flashlight, so this is the moment to go over to her and climb up onto the path.

---

Artefact #2: Smuggler Note

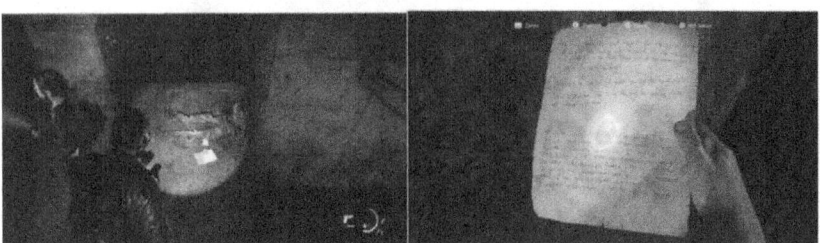

Next to the corpse where Ellie finds the flashlight, there's an Artefact named Smuggler Note.

Firefly Pendant #2: Jiang's Firefly Pendant

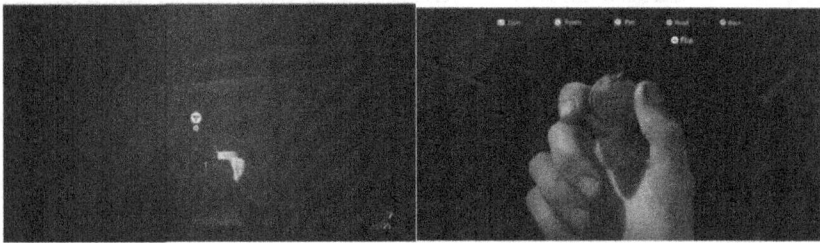

Immediately ahead of the previous Artefact, go down the stairs and into the water. Dive under the water and stay beneath the surface into the room at the back. Among the shelves is a Firefly Pendant named Jiang's Firefly Pendant, as well as some Weapon Parts. You can also get some Supplements on the ledge directly above.

---

Once you're done, return to Ellie and swim to the far left. Grab the wooden panel, and swim back to Ellie with it so she can climb aboard. Then carry her to the other side and wait for her to drop the ladder into the water.

Climb up the ladder, out of the water, and follow the pathway to a staircase which leads you out of the subway. A cutscene will trigger, as you make your way to The Woods.

# BILL'S TOWN

## The Woods

You are now out in the woods. Head forward to get to a trail. If you want some supplies, look down by the grate to your right in the riverbed. To the right of the grate along the path is some enhancement pills. Once further down the trail, you get to the base of a water tower.

Move around the left of the fence to find a plank. Grab it and move the plank so that it is leaning against the building directly behind it. Now go find the air conditioning unit and climb on here, then get on top of the building. There is a modified melee weapon up here, so be sure to pick it up.

Now pull up the plank, then lay it across the gap to clear the fence. Drop down here and move past the water tower down a hill. You see a break in the fence here, so go through into the town ahead. There is a Clicker in the shed straight in front of you, so go around and up the metal stairs to the side door of a building.

*Artifact 18: Pills Note*

There is a room up here with some computers in it as well as this artifact.

If you are feeling brave, go downstairs, take out the Clicker in the shed, and pick up the item on the shelf. There is another Clicker in the area, so kill him too if you want. Once you're done in the area, drop down next to those metal stairs. Open the shiv door on the left for a bunch of items. Boost Ellie up and over the fence, and then move through the gate. Once over fence you can't return.

There are lots of goodies around, especially back by the garden area. There are a few supplies in the pizza shop as well.

Optional Conversation 7: When walking into the pizza shop Ellie will notice a arcade machine, which will prompt an optional conversation.

There are a bunch of parts near the blue dumpster behind the pizza shop. There are also a few parts up the stairs next to the pizza shop.

Firefly Pendant 8: Climb up onto the RV to get a Firefly Pendant.

*Artifact 19: Note to Bob*

Farther down past the RV, there is a wall blocking the street. On the barbed wire, there is this artifact.

Once you are finished, head back down the road towards the pizza shop, on your left before the pizza shop will be a pick up truck and safe. Open the safe. It contains ammo, items, and other supplies, then go back in the record store.

*Artifact 20: Perimeter Note*

In the back office of the record store, you can find this artifact on the desk.

Now go behind the record store. You will see some of Bill's traps in action, so keep your eyes peeled for more of them. There is an unlockable door back here that you can use a shiv to open.

There are lots of goodies in here to grab. Heading back outside behind the buildings, you see a man shot dead with arrows. snag the arrows then go down the stairs to grab the ladder. Lean it up against the back of the truck here, then climb on up. The Bow is up on the top of the truck with another arrow.

Cross the beam onto the roof and climb up the ladder here to reach the rooftops. It's too far a jump to make it to the next roof, so go back to grab that beam and bring it up to the rooftops to stretch across the gap.

Kill the Clicker in front of you, then keep moving across the rooftops towards the Church and the smoke. Drop down from the ladder back to the street then duck under Bill's trap.

There is a door down here that is being beaten on from the inside, so go over and open it up! There are supplies on the left before the stairs. Take the stairs up and head to the bedroom for more supplies. There is one Runner as you go through to the kitchen.

*Artifact 21: Note to Rachel*

After you take care of the Runner, this note can be found on the table in the room.

After you have picked up the artifact, grab the supplements from the bathroom.

Go down the alley and use bottles or pistol to take out the two trip wires. Open door in warehouse to exit area and get ready for a cut scene.

**Safehouse**

After the drama of that cutscene (Ellie's got a bit of a pottymouth), you are now safe for a bit. Get all the supplies you can in the restaurant.

*Artifact 22: Bill's Map*

If you remember from the cutscene, Bill pointed out the location on the map. Retrieve the map from the same table that was on the cutscene.

*Artifact 23: Fences Note*

There is a small room in here. In the room on the coffee table, you can find this artifact.

Training Manual 1: Shiv Sharpening

Check the bar, you can find this manual lying on the counter. (Note: If you're on New Game Plus, you probably picked this up on your last playthrough, and it won't be there).

Optional Conversation 8: Go to the chess board on one of the tables of one of the booths for a optional conversation about chess with Ellie.

Once done, go over to Bill, who will let you out the back way. Follow him upstairs, and collect the supplies up here.

*Artifact 24: Hunters Note*

Turn right at the top of the stairs and there will be a kitchen, this will be on a table in here.

Once ready, follow Bill out behind the building sign and into another window. Move through this apartment then down the stairs into a diner. Watch as Bill empties one of his traps, then head outside to the street.

Right outside you get ambushed by a decent amount of Infected. eliminate them all.

Firefly Pendant 9: Look up at the light posts down the street, one of them will have a firefly pendant. Throw a brick or bottle to get it.

Follow Bill across the street through a gate, check the shed for some stuff ( not on grounded difficulty). Then head up some stairs. Once up the stairs, run to your left, you will find a bundle of ten parts. Head over to the cellar door and go on in. You now have the Shotgun.

Go talk to Bill to get one of his Nail Bombs. There are tons of supplies in this basement, including "tools," so collect everything you can find. There's also a bench down here if you want to build anything. Once your ready to head out, follow Bill up the stairs into the Church.

*Artifact 25: Bombs Note*

There is a room to the right as you get closer to Bill. When you go in, Bill will tell you it's his room. On his desk you can find this artifact.

**Graveyard**

Once you're ready to take off from the Church, head over to Bill and follow him out of a window in the back of the Church. It's stealth time now, as there are a bunch of Clickers in the cemetary. It's pretty easy to have any approach here, stealth killing, sneaking, or gunz-a-blazin.

Once you make it down to the bottom of the cemetary, head out the gate here towards the school. This is another section where stealth will be your friend. Make sure you have some shivs to take out Clickers. There are also regular Runners as well, so be prepared to also strangle people and have a finger on your trigger if your stealth plan goes arseways.

There are 3 infected in the yard to the right.

Firefly Pendant 10: Inside the house's laundry room next to the kitchen there is a firefly pendant.

You will come up on a garage on your left. Go in the garage, then out the door in the garage to keep moving forward. The door is tied, so rip off the doggy-door cover and let Ellie crawl through. Head out of the garage now, but be ready for more Clickers in the house. TIP: If you flank right, you can see them by the patio door, one well placed Molotov will dispatch of them all!

Once you clear out the house, there are very few supplies. Listen to what Bill says here, how you are just going to get in, get the battery, and run out as fast as possible. Head outside and up on the RV to make it into the treehouse. Once you're up here, drop down into the yard next door with the pool.

The school is on the other side of this house and there are no infected around. Loot the shed out back and the house as there are lots of supplies here.

*Artifact 26: Boy's Diary*

If you go to the second floor, there is a boy's room with this artifact by the window.

Optional Conversation 9: As you leave, Ellie enters the room and asks if you can talk.

Once you feel you have fully looted the house, step into the garage and help Bill lift up the garage door. Sneak or blast your way through the Infected here, then get to a bus that you can boost Ellie up on. Once she's up there, she'll knock down a ladder to help you and Bill climb up. Follow Bill around the school as he discovers that the school door is locked. He'll find an open window, so follow him in - Just in time!

## High School Escape

Uh oh, your plan to get the battery has failed. Follow Bill through the school now. There are some supplies on the landing of the stairs at the first encounter. Stealth kill your way through the hall into what looks like a science classroom. Work your way through the back of the room and out into a different hallway.

You make your way to a door that is blocked. Push your way through and a super scary Infected comes into the gym. He's a Bloater, so use Molotovs to really mess with him, then follow through with a Shotgun. Do NOT try to be stealthy! Once dead, head over to the room the Bloater came from and get a few supplies and parts before boosting Bill up to the top of the bleachers.

After Bill and Ellie get up, three Runners come attack you. Kill them then get pulled up to the bleachers as well. Jump out of the window, then back down to the ground.

Run through the hole in the fence, then climb up the ladder against the wooden fence. After all that, loot the house; check 'bedroom' and kitchen.

*Artifact 27: Note from Frank*

In the bedroom, on the desk there is this artifact. Grabbing this artifact activates an optional conversation with Bill.

Optional Conversation 10: After you retrieved the previous artifact, go to Bill and you will be able to give him the note.

*Artifact 28: Note from Frank (Crumpled)*

After Bill reads the note and crumples it, and throws it to the ground. Go retrieve it. Yes, it counts as another collectible.

Optional Conversation 11: There is also a conversation with Ellie as she sits in the driver's seat.

Once ready, get behind the truck and push. Ellie doesn't get the clutch to pop the first time, so quickly get behind the truck and push again. Infected will start coming at you, so act quickly. You will have to push and stop a few times to get to the hill at the end of the street. Once there, run and hop into the bed of the truck to drive off.

# PITTSBURGH

### Alone and Forsaken
Artifact 29: Siphon Hose

Bill gives this to Joel in the previous cutscene.

Comic 1: Force Carrier

You will also have this collectible from the beginning of the chapter because Ellie stole it from Bill in the previous chapter.

After slamming into the hardware store, be ready to follow the onscreen prompts. Once you have taken full control of Joel again, go save Ellie! After beating down those thugs who jump you, take out the other ones (the rifle is particularly useful here since there is a long shooting gallery). Then loot the store [under cash register and soda machine, health bar by extinguisher in center of room] and the garage office [in the front table and in locker & 2 desks of office], and find a garage door to lift up and sneak under.

Looting this room includes Level 2 tools, a Smoke grenade, and some supplies in a locker.

Optional Conversation 12: Make your way over to Ellie as you enter, you will be able to initiate an optional conversation when she stops by a pile.

Artifact 30: Tourists Manifest

In the right corner of the room, you can find this on the tipped over cabinet.

Once ready, find the door on the left and move on out.

Head up the stairs, then through the door. Loot the sleeping area up here.

Training Manual 2: Health Splinting

Near the middle of the room, on the rack near the mattress you can find this manual.

Once looted, go through the blue door at the end of the hallway to find more supplies, an Artifact (the Ambush Map), and a crafting bench.

Artifact 31: Ambush Map

On the wall in the room with the workbench, you can find it on the wall by the door you entered the room by.

Once ready, head back out to the hallway and find the gray door along the wall to go through. Once back outside, head up the metal stairs, then drop down to meet up with Ellie. You are now back on street-level. Turn left, immediately, for some weapons parts, then directly across from the drop to street level are some upgrade pills and gun parts.

Comic 2: Termination Shock

There is a crashed bus ahead, towards the back of inside of the bus you can find this comic on the floor.

Optional Conversation 13: Meet back up with Ellie and have a conversation by the body that appears to have fallen out of the car.

Now continue down the street. Take cover, because three enemies show up. Let them wander down the street until you either want to take them out or they are out of range. Once clear, run over to the military zone where the crashed bus is.

Ellie's Jokes 01: Wait near the car by the bus until Ellie pulls out her joke book to tell you some jokes (Required for the That's All I Got Trophy). Push triangle to start her off and listen to her jokes. Note, it can take a while for her to get her book, so be patient and stand still.

Climb up onto a car then get to the top of the crashed bus blocking your way. Drop down by the military checkpoint, and go all the way to the right to find some gun parts.

Optional Conversation 14: After dropping down, to the right there is graffiti on the wall. When Ellie starts to talk about it, you can initiate an optional conversation afterwards.

Artifact 32: Lost Hill Note

After the conversation, jump over the sandbags and just under the counter in the guard booth, this artifact will be on the ground.

The Last of Us Remastered Grounded Walkthrough Part 12: Alone and Forsaken No Damage All Collectibles

Once you have looted the area, continue through the checkpoint. You hear a few Hunters ahead, so use your focused hearing to get an idea of where they are at. You should take them out as you are about to get into some kind of enemy outpost. There are A LOT of enemies in this book store (2 floors).

The best bet would be to sneak around taking out every enemy you see. If Hunters see you, there are plenty of brick and bottles for distractions and places to hide behind to make them all walk around cluelessly.

Once you have taken out the last Hunter, loot the book store. There are tons of nooks and crannies to find hidden goodies in here.

Ellie's Jokes 02: Go by the cafe and wait for a minute, Ellie will pull out her joke book again. Push triangle to start her off and listen to her jokes. All enemies need to be eliminated for this to work.

Artifact 33: Lost Areas Map

To the right of the counter, there is a shiv door. Behind the shiv door you can find this artifact locked away, as well as some pills, 5 parts, and some other items.

Artifact 34: Abandon Zone Note

In one of the office like areas on the ground floor of the bookstore (the right side of the store), you can find this on a desk.

Artifact 35: Applicant Checklist

From the entrance of the bookstore, turn right and you will see a set of stairs. Under those stairs, you can find this artifact hidden in the darkness.

Firefly Pendant 11: In the alley in the far end of the bookstore area, you can find this behind the tipped shelf.

Artifact 36: Traitors Flyer

Around where you first entered the bookstore area before you encountered the Hunters, there are walls in front of the bookstore. If you are facing the front of the bookstore, turn right and you should be able to see it plastered on the wall.

Once ready to move on, head up to the second floor and find the double doors with the EXIT sign over them. Go on through here and down the stairs to keep moving towards the bridge. There are a couple of supplies under the stairs you came down. Follow the street, past the strung up soldiers, go up the metal stairs then drop down onto the truck Look for upgrade parts to the right of the truck to the left and back some there are some supplements as well. Go down the alley until you are out on a major street.

Looks like the coast is clear now, so go loot the area.

Optional Conversation 15: Spin 180 degrees and walk away from the cab and look to your right, you will see advertisments on the wall, one of a model. Ellie will ask you about her.

Ellie's Jokes 03: After Ellie has stopped talking, she will walk about for a while, and eventually get out her joke book.

Continue back, with the model on your right to find some crafting ingredients. Then wait a minute and she will pull out her joke book again. There's a door with a red X to the left of the cab that you can use a shiv to get open. There's plenty of loot in there (arrows, revolver rounds, 50 gun parts, rifle rounds, 15 upgrade pills, tape, bandage, and scissors) as well as an artifact (Mother's Letter) on the chair when you first walk in.

Artifact 37: Mother's Letter

As mentioned above, in the room behind the shiv door you can locate this artifact on the chair.

Back out on the street now, get into the water and swim over by the road overpass. Some big tank thing drives by, but you can ignore it for now. Grab the wood pallet (dive under for 10 parts) and bring it over for Ellie to sit on. Float her over to the bus where you saw those Hunters.

She will get off and extend a bridge, so you need to go into the back of the semi truck here.

Artifact 38: Stash Note

Go through the truck to get into a cafe. Get out of the water and loot the cafe, including going up to the second floor. There are lots of items here (including a shiv) as well as an Artifact (Stash Note...which tells you about the room you just looted, yay).

Once looted, go back to the first floor and get on top of the semi trailer now. Walk across the bridge and into the hotel.

**Hotel Lobby**
The lobby is clear, so search all over looting it. To the left side of the entrance

(construction area), you'll find the ladder. Walk past the ladder. There is a cafe with some supplies and a coffee maker.

Note: Before doing anything else, there is an unlisted optional conversation with Ellie: as soon as you enter the lobby, head right and stand behind the counter. After the game gives you an L3 notification that you'll need to go upstairs, Elllie will walk up to the counter and joke around about her luggage...worth the wait. If you grab the ladder before this conversation, it will be unavailable (Added 18 July 17).

Optional Conversation 16: Go near the coffee maker for an optional comment from Joel.

Pick up the ladder and carry it over toward the staircase, but on the way stop and prop it up on the other side of the scaffold you took it from. There is 10 parts up there. Now look across, there is a break in the hand rail, jump down and prop the ladder there and climb on up.

At the top of the ladder, turn right and go down the lobby stairs, you can inch your way back up the other side.

Artifact 39: Note to Staff

There's an Artifact up here that gives you the combination to the safe. After you climb the ladder, on the right is a passage you can shimmy by to retrieve this artifact in the suitcase. Hop the railing and head left to the front desk. There's a 5 pill bottle, some ingredients, and the safe. Open the safe in the room behind the front desk.

Training Manual 3: Shiv Reinforcement

In the safe, there is a training manual that lets you make three stabs with a shiv before it breaks, along with 50 parts, and some ammo and ingredients.

Head back up the ladder now.

Ellie's Jokes 04: Once back up the ladder, stand still and wait for Ellie to pull out her joke book a fourth time.

Head out through a window (from one of the many trailers) and hear some more Hunters in the area. Be on your guard now as you sneak into the window across the clearing now. You are now in the actual hotel area where all the rooms are.

Hunters abound here so take whatever approach you would like. TONS of items scattered here, but it requires a lot of hunting. It's best to take out all of the enemies first, then roam the hallways unhindered.

Once ready, head up the staircase to the next floor. There are more Hunters up here. Take out the guys up on this floor and loot everything again.

Optional Conversation 17: In one room are people in a tub that sparks a short conversation with Ellie.

There's also 5 upgrade pills in the vanity behind the tub people and a hole in the wall leading to a blocked off room with ingredients under that bathroom's sink and 10 gun parts in the adjoining bedroom (with a big hole in the floor). Check out the balcony to get a "great" view of the desolation of Pittsburgh, then head inside and loot the bed dresser for some gun parts. Take the other staircase up now, and find an elevator. Mash Triangle to force the doors open, then climb up the ladder. Shimmy around the fence then drop down to the other elevator. Boost Ellie up the ledge to the open door, then take a quick plunge.

Immediately dive straight down to pick up several weapon tool parts. Then, swim forward to get to a room with three possible exits. The one to the left involves opening a door. That is NOT the right way to go, as evidenced by the massive piles of rubble that rain down. Going through the open double doors on the right nets you a few supplies, but is not the way to keep moving forward. Let's try going straight ahead now.

Looks like we will have to dive down the flooded stairway. Swim down through a door into a room with a few floating bodies. Very creepy, but you have to ignore them and keep going if you don't want to drown. Through another door here into a room where you can surface and breath. There is a door off to the right side with a few supplies in it. Find the door with the sign above it saying "West Tower B1" and dive down in the water until you can swim through the door under it.

You pop out in the staff locker room. Move out into the hallway, and Joel will put on his gasmask. Keep going until you find a door to the right. There's a generator in here, so wait to power it up. To move forward, you need to find the access card. The best way to do this is to head upstairs and find it before starting the generator. If you go up the rubble ramp next to the generator and turn around there is a door at the far end of the room and one to the right of it. Head through the door on the right and go straight across the hall into the security room to snag the access card.

Artifact 40: Hotel Keycard

The access card here is an artifact, since this is story driven, this artifact can't be missed.

Now go back downstairs and power on the generator. Maybe that wasn't the best idea. A bunch of Runners and a Bloater will show up, so arm yourself. Either run upstairs to try to avoid the Infected or stand and fight them all. Either way, you need to get to a door upstairs that is locked. It's all the way to the left once you get to the second floor. Swipe the card in the reader, then head through the door.

Go up the stairs and through that door to a hallway. There's a bench here if you want to craft any upgrades. After looting all the rooms and building your upgrades, head out the door at the end of the hall. You come up on a kitchen with a Clicker in the distance. Some Hunters get into the kitchen and take out the Clicker, but then start scanning the rest of the kitchen for more Infected.

Take them all out however you would like. Make sure to stop in the freezer for some supplies too. Once you make it to the front of the dining room, there is a ladder on the ground. Pick it up and prop it up against the wall directly in front of you. Climb on up to get kicked right back down. Good thing Ellie has your back, right? Time to get out of here.

Climb back up the ladder, this time not getting kicked off. Move through the conference room, but duck back into the dining room again.

Comic 3: Accretion

Shimmy along the ledge to get over to the bar area. There are a few supplies here, and the comic is on the table by the couches. Snag everything, then head back to Ellie.

Go down the stairs here and drop down to the lower level.

Firefly Pendant 12: There's a women's restroom here to the left, so go in here to find a Firefly Pendant.

Go back into the hallway.

Training Manual 4: Melee Knots

A little farther down to find a Training Manual on a table.

Go forward now, jumping over a table in the way to get to a ballroom.

Optional Conversation 18: Head over to the beach back drop and start an optional conversation with Ellie.

On the stage, push the piano over against the wall. Use it as a stepping stone to climb up. Once up here, move towards the open door, then the double doors. Climb out onto the scaffolding.

## Financial District

After finding out that these Hunters know of your presence, let's mess with them some more. Head off to the left after the group finishes talking, and take out a Hunter here.

Sneak into the bank and take out a second. Now, sneak your way through the courtyard taking out enemies as you go. A good way to do this is to go back to where you started, then go to the other side into Rivers Cafe. Move upstairs and take out the guard up here, then continue to take out enemies.

Artifact 41: Fireflies Note

On the right of the area is a sub shop. In the freezer in the back you can find this artifact.

There are two "waves" kinda, so after clearing out the first, start on the second. You cannot take them all out without being seen, so make sure you have the guns you want loaded. After taking out the last guard, there will be a cutscene.

Optional Conversation 19: Around the beginning of the area, by the closest tree on the left there will be a body hanging from it. Stay there long enough and Ellie will come over and look at it, starting an optional conversation.

Loot the courtyard area now, then move to the back by the RV. Go over to the garage door and lift it up to move on.

Grab the cart that Ellie used to hold open the door and drag it over to the window. Climb on up and over to find a work bench you can build upgrades at.

Hop over the downed table to see some really messed up stuff. Now head out the door and go up the stairs. You hear two Hunters coming, so either hide behind the small wall across from the stairwell and let them pass or go back downstairs and take cover. Depending on the optinon you chose, you can leave them be or take out the Hunters, then go upstairs and all the way down the hallway.

Artifact 42: Final Attack Note

Under a desk up here, you can find this artifact.

A rubble ramp leads from up here back down to the street.

The Last of Us Remastered Grounded Walkthrough Part 15: Financial District No Damage All Collectibles

Move down the street until you get to an intersection. There are Hunters up in the second floor of a building across the street. There are also grenade traps around, so make sure you look where you are going. Sneak across the street to the building where the Hunters are. Go up the stairs and take out the two guards up here.

Artifact 43: Mob Attack Note

There is a large desk with a computer on it and behind it, there is this artifact.

Make your way down the stairs now, and eliminate the few remaining Hunters over by the tank.

Artifact 44: Truck Note

In the credit union/ration depot, there is this artifact on top of a desk in here as well as a shiv door to open.

Loot the building, then head back across the street to the fire escapes. Boost Ellie up then climb up the ladder she knocks down. Make your way across the fire escape until you can drop down onto a truck on the other side of the wall. You're getting close to the bridge now.

Note: Just before you boost Ellie up the fire escape ladder, there are four or five soldiers that have been killed against a brick wall. There is a conversation prompt, but apparently it doesn't count towards your Optional Conversation count. You don't need to talk to Ellie in this instance to receive the trophy.

Optional Conversation 20: Ellie will talk about the military prep school here.

Optional Conversation 21: Behind you is a large movie poster (Dawn of the Wolf: Part 2) which Ellie will talk about while Joel reminiscence.

Move on down the alley until you hear some voices and the humvee. Get into stealth mode and slowly make your way down the alley until you pass the building. There's a Hunter on the side of the building, so stealth kill him. Sneak along the side of the building now and run into the bush outside of the side door.

This will alert a Hunter, so hide in the bush until he comes out, then stealth kill him. Take out the last guy in the store with stealth now, then go back to the side of the building. Sneak from behind the van to behind the police car, then across the street.

There are two more Hunters in this building across the street, so take them out while avoiding line of sight with the Humvee. Loot the back room, then move down the back alley behind the store. Take out the Hunted and keep going until you find an open door on the left. The Humvee may come chasing you back here, so quickly run into the building then up the stairs to the second floor. Head out the window to the fire escape, and go up a floor. Cross over the wood plank bridge and shimmy along the building ledge until you can hop into a bedroom window.

Loot this apartment, then hop out the window by the fridge. Shimmy down along the building until you find another window with a curtain blowing out the side. Jump in to see what's going on.

After meeting Henry and Sam, loot the apartment. There's a decent amount of goodies here

Training Manual 5: Molotov Construction

The highlist of goodies is the manual on the kitchen counter.

Once ready, head down the stairs following the group.

Comic 4: Deep Phase

One floor down, there is a shiv door. Inside there are a ton of supplies but in the kids' bedroom, you'll find this comic on the chair.

Now follow Henry and Sam back down the stairs. After going through the toy store, you come out to find three Hunters in the parking lot. Take them out, then climb from the car to the truck to the top of the building on the left. Once you get to the first roof, take cover because two more Hunters come out.

Take them out, and jump up to the next roof section where they came from.

Firefly Pendant 13: Once across and into the building, check out the Mens bathroom to find a Firefly Pendant.

Now head across the hallway through the door that Henry is holding open. You are now in the offices of an architecture firm.

Artifact 45: Trial Note

In the conference room with the big table, you can find this artifact on the ground in the corner.

There isn't much in the rest of the office, so move through it until Henry unlocks the door to the CEO's office.

### Escape the City

Time to take out that night-time skeleton crew. Follow Henry out of the office now and down the stairs to street level. You and him will both sneak up on the two Hunters standing by the fire and stealth kill both.

Now head out the side door. You need to stick to the shadows, so don't go near the spotlight. Stick to the right side and make sure to take cover behind concrete barriers to not be seen. When close enough, turn off the generator, killing the search light.

Now, prepare to hide or stand and take on the Hunters who drop down. Once all taken care of, head over to the big door they were guarding, and rush inside. There's one more Hunter here, but Henry can take him out really quickly. Go over to the semi trailer and boost Ellie up to the half ladder at the top.

Well, that WOULD have been a good plan. Henry is such a jerk. Run over to the big garage door and quickly interact with it to get inside away from the Humvee. Moving around in here, you come out in an Irish Pub. Take out the handful of Hunted in here, then grab the cart blocking the front door. Move it out of the way, and head out the front door.

The Humvee is coming now, so RUUUUN!!! Keep running as fast as you can until you have to jump over a barrier by a bus.

## THE SUBURBS

### Sewers

Artifact 46: Boat Note

Climb aboard and open up the main cabin door to find this artifact on the dash.

Comic 5: Antiparticles

Right next to the note is this comic book.

There may also be other supplies in the main cabin.

Firefly Pendant 14: Go on the deck, and drop through the hole to find the Firefly Pendant of Josh Soheffler behind a fishing net.

When you are ready, climb up the rocks by the waterfall to get to a sewer grate. Yank it off with Triangle to get through. Head forward through the sewer.

Firefly Pendant 15: There will be a small space you can crawl through on the right, so go in there to find a dead end and a Firefly Pendant.

Head back out to the main sewer again, and you come up on a fork. The two guys take the left way, so go right. You come up on a caged area, but the door is blocked. Look at the floor for a grate to rip off the wall. Ellie can crawl through here and open up the door.

Artifact 47: Sewers Note

In the room that Ellie opened up, you can find this on the table as well as other supplies in here.

Cut through the tunnel directly across the hallway from the cage to meet back up with the guys. Head through the door up here now, and continue down the sewer. You come across a large room that is mostly flooded.

Firefly Pendant 16: There is a car here, so go dive by it to find a Firefly Pendant.

Now swim over to the huge door and pull out the pipe that is blocking the door from opening. Henry cranks open the door the full way now, so swim through.

Climb up the ladder and you will hear some familiar and unwelcome sounds. Go to the left of this walkway to toss a wood pallet over into the water. Head over to the door now, and open it up. Eliminate the two Clickers.

Artifact 48: Trading Note

In the back corner of the room near a mattress, you can find this on the ground.

Move back to the water, and swim with the pallet over to Ellie. Let her hop on and swim her over to the little waterfall area here. She'll hop out, power up the generator, and pull the two men over. Now hop out with the help of Henry and continue down the sewer.

There's a small room on the left here with a few supplies as well as Level 3 tools, so stock up then head over to what looks like a castle drawn with chalk. Head through the door and find a lot of awesome things.

First, you find a sawed off shotgun on a table, so get that for a new weapon.

Training Manual 6: Bomb Containment

There is a manual on the bottom shelf over here.

Move down the hallway here now until you get to a door. Once through the door, a group of Infected attack including a Clicker, so fight them all off.

Artifact 49: Rain Catcher Note

Once clear, head up the stairs here to get to a few more supplies and an Artifact.

Go back down now, and hop the barrier to continue forward.

Artifact 50: Cornered Note

Check out the door to the left to find more supplies and another Artifact.

Move forward and open a gated door to trigger a trap.

Ellie and Henry have run off to protect themselves, so now you need to go do the same. There are lots of infected in this room. They are mostly Runners and one or two Clickers. Take them all out, then loot the area. There's plenty of supplies around, so don't be stingy.

Artifact 51: Kid's Drawing

You eventually come across a "classroom" with lots of Children's toys and things like that. There's an Artifact here, so grab it.

Then boost Sam up a ledge to knock down a ladder.

You move up the ladder and into the next room to see some familiar faces. Yay! Oh wait, RUN!!! Start sprinting forward until you get into a room with a blocked door. Sam will crawl through a tunnel to open the door, so keep going. Run up the stairs and drop down to get to a cleared room. Loot it then go open the door. Oh, it's blocked. Ellie and Sam go above the door through the window to unjam the door, so you and Henry have to stand your guard. Be ready to fight some Infected. Once the door is clear, run through it.

**Suburbs**

You are now outside. Continue forward with the group, stopping to pick up the supplies in the back of the van. Move forward to see the radio tower as you approach a town. Walk along the road until you find a brick house you can go in.

Artifact 52: Looting Note

Head in and loot all three floors. There's an Artifact up on the third floor in one of the bedrooms.

When you're ready, head back out the front door and continue down the road.

If you're going for the trophy about Ellie's jokes and optional conversations, first go into the kitchen of the house with the "U LOOT I SHOOT" warning and listen to Henry's spiel on barbeque.

Optional Conversation 22: Next, go across the street to the house with the warning "I'M ARMED NO TRESPASSING" and be ready to answer Henry when he asks you a question.

Optional Conversation 23: Moving forward, follow Ellie and Sam to the ice cream truck and answer Ellie's question. Go back a little bit and you'll come across a garage with a workbench in it. Construct any upgrades that you can, then continue to the next house.

This one is also made out of brick. Head in to resupply.

Artifact 53: Father's Note

On the second floor in the master bedroom, this can be found on the dresser.

Training Manual 7: Melee Techniques

In the area upstairs, there is an attic. Pull down the ladder to the attic from here and boost Ellie up into it. She'll pull down a Training Manual to make your melee weapons stronger.

Move onto the next house now (blue siding) as the dogs run away when you get close.

Artifact 54: Survivors Note

There's an Artifact up on the second floor again (by the computer).

Comic 6: Messenger Particle

There is also a comic book in the bathroom.

Artifact 55: Matchbook

Head up to the attic to find a matchbook that has a safe combination written in it. Go back down a floor into a bedroom to unlock the safe and get more supplies.

Optional Conversation 24: When you go downstairs you see the kids playing darts, after they have finish you have a go at darts.

Ellie's Jokes 05: Once all 4 optional conversations have been activated in this area, go to the dead end at the very end of the road, and wait for Ellie to wander around until she pulls out her joke book for the final time.

Firefly Pendant 17: In the backyard after Ellie tells her joke, in the tree above the swingset that hangs from a tree branch.

Go back through the blue sided house and now head to the back yard when you are ready. Take the stairs back here to continue toward the radio tower.

You drop down and immediately get shot at. Not a nice thing to happen. Joel is going to go take out the sniper while everyone else hangs back to distract him. There are tons of ways to approach this area, but one thing to keep in mind is that being stealthy is really hard.

The Hunters here are all looking for you, and will attack immediately on sight. All of the houses have supplies in them. You can climb up the wall to the left and hop through the window of the first house. If you hide behind the kitchen counter, you can take out one of the hunters stealthily. But watch out, there are plenty more around the corner. The broken house at the end also has some supplies on the upper floor.

You can also take the path over to the right. A good strategy is to wait until the sniper has fired a shot, then sprint to the next cover and wait for the next shot. Be aware that the sniper can shoot through open windows in the houses. This applies especially to the first two houses on the right. The last house on the right has supplies underneath the outdoor stairway (right side). Crouch to crawl underneath. There is also an open kitchen on the other side that you can only access from the side facing the sniper.

Whichever way you choose (or both!), make your way to the house at the end of the street with the sniper. Once in the house, head up to the third floor and into the room with the sniper. Keep in mind that once you have entered the sniper's nest, you will no longer be able to explore the area for supplies. Fight him off, then take a turn with his weapon yourself.

You now have to protect your friends. This sniper section is decently long, so don't worry about ammo. There is an infinite supply. Also, don't worry about headshots, as any shot that lands is an insta-kill.

Take out all of the Hunters until the Tank shows back up again. Wait for the driver to pop out of the top with a Molotov and shoot him to light up the whole tank. This causes some Infected to show up, and by "some" I mean a TON. Take them out by providing cover for everyone else. Once they get to the house you are in, you all make the smart choice to simply book it.

# TOMMY'S DAM

### Hydroelectric Dam

Start off by walking forward now into Jackson County. The road you are on crumbles at the end.

The El Diablo pistol is location near the open driver's door of the rusting law enforcement jeep. There's some alcohol and nail/scissor parts lying on the road behind the trunk.

Follow the "path" until you are in the river bed. Move down the river, jumping over rocks that are in your way.

Comic 7: Foreign Element

Before heading under the bridge towards the hydroelectric plant, on a hill to your right is a rusted up car, and a collectable comic for Ellie.

Once done, head over to the plant and go up the stairs and use a shiv to get through the door.

Loot the room, then head over to the wheel next to the dam. Turn it to raise half of the improvised bridge, then hop over the rail that is upriver to walk around the side of the building. Dive in the water and swim down until you find a sunken building. In the roof is a wood palate that you can kick free.

Use the pallet to bring Ellie to the other side of the dam. She'll turn the wheel on this side, so go back to where you came from and walk across the newly formed bridge. Jump off the walkway and check out the abandoned camp site.

Optional Conversation 25: High five Ellie then walk over to the grave marked with a teddybear to talk with Ellie.

Now turn around and climb up the rocks. You come up sandwiched between a fence and the power plant wall. Go over to the outpost to find some supplies and an artifact. There are also some supplements behind the bulldozer.

Artifact 56: Power Plant Map

In the same outpost with the supplies, you find this pinned to the wall in there.

When ready, try to open the power plant doors. After that touching reunion, walk along with everyone until you get to the building.

Optional Conversation 26: There is an optional conversation with Ellie about horses while she's petting one and you can also pet the horse yourself.

Now you are working with Tommy. He has something to show you, so go talk to him. Move upstairs and head to the left into a room with some supplements and parts then head back out and follow Tommy to the center of the Power Plant.

Optional Conversation 27: On the outside platform, before you head into the center, is a woman with a rifle with whom you can have an optional conversation.

Training Manual 8: Smoke Chemistry

There's a Training manual on the counter by the main console, so grab it to make your smokescreens last twice as long.

There's a work bench over here too, so build any upgrades you want. Go into the turbine room, and watch as power gets restored to the facility.

Firefly Pendant 18: Walk down here and go into a door under the room you were just in. There's some supplies and a Firefly Pendant in here.

When you are ready, follow Tommy through the far door in the turbine room.

You guys are under attack now! Fight your way through the turbine room and out back where you just came from.

Artifact 57: Plant Schematics

Make sure to grab the Artifact on the table in the control room before leaving.

Fight your way across the bridge and then into the other building. Kill all of the men who are attacking. You are now on a horse chasing down Ellie.

Follow Tommy to a dead end, then go back a bit to where a trail leads off of the main road. Follow Tommy and the trail down here until you jump over a log and get attacked. Kill all of the Hunters down here, then hop back on your horses.

Jump over the log with barbed wire at the top to continue down the path. Keep going until you get to a ranch.

**Ranch House**

Get close to the front door and hop off your horse using Triangle. Loot the first floor of the house here.

Firefly Pendant 19: There is a pendant on a desk (on the first floor).

Once ready, head upstairs.

Comic 8: Zero Point

There's a Comic in the bedroom left at the top of the stairs.

Keep looting the rest of the rooms, even though they don't have anything too special.

Open the door at the end of the hallway now to find Ellie. Two Hunters are now on the second floor with three downstairs. Hide in the bedroom until one walks into the bathroom. Take him out, then let the second guy walk past and take him out as well. Now, move downstairs. Go really slowly until they break off into rooms. Take out the one to the right, in the kitchen, first. Then move across the hall and take the other two out. Now head out the front door to get to the horses.

# THE UNIVERSITY

### Go Big Horns
Comic 9: Free Radicals

Instead of going through the gate, head all the way back up the street to get to a Comic.

There are also 10 supplements hidden behind the car found at the end of the street.

Now head onto the campus. There is a building to the right that has an open garage. Head in here to find the Flame Thrower!

Artifact 58: Sniper's Nest Log

There is also tons of supplies, a bench in the garage to build upgrades, and an Artifact up two flights of stairs.

Once you are ready to head out, get back on the horse to hop over the barriers lined with barbed wire.

Optional Conversation 28: After clearing the hurdle, on the top of the building to the left is a Big Horns banner that you can have a conversation with Ellie about.

Once up the street into the clearing, the only way to go will be through the gaping hole in the building on the left.

Firefly Pendant 20: But first, go to your right, there will be a firefly pendant up in the yellow tree. Don't waste your bullets, throw one of the nearby bottles to knock it down.

Head back to the hole in the wall and move down the hallway to a closed gate.

Go through the gate to hear some Runners. Ellie and the horse stay back, so move forward.

Artifact 59: Wall Panel Note

Off to the right is a metal gate that has been tampered with, grab the note next to the gate's control panel.

Sneak your way up the stairs leading back the way you came. Move down the hall until you get to a walkway. Now be super sneaky. There are five runners up here, so take them out however you wish (that new Flame Thrower is pretty fun here if you want to ignore stealth.) Once all clear, power up the generator and head on out the door with Ellie. Head up the flight of stairs and get back on the horse to clear the barbed wire barrier here.

Firefly Pendant 21: Before jumping the barbed barrier, to the right there is building with a small opening. Climb on up and you will find a Firefly Pendant.

You are now in the center of campus. There will be a group of monkeys by the football field, but they run away when you get close. Facing the statue at the center of the courtyard, to the right is Ding Hall where you will find an opening in the building exposing a stairway. Go up the flight of stairs, then jump out the window onto the roof.

Training Manual 9: Health Sterilization

Hop back in a window to find supplies and a Training Manual that upgrades your health kits to be 67% stronger.

Continue to loot the area for pills and guns parts.

There's also some supplies hidden in the open container in front of the building, Ding Hall.

Continue forward on the ground now, going through a tunnel to get behind the big building here.

Optional Conversation 29: When you enter the campus square and see the monkeys, Ding Hall will be on your right. If you go over in that direction and then head left, you'll pass between two buildings. The first Firefly symbol is on your left, and the symbol you want to use is straight ahead. Initiate it to talk to Ellie about the Fireflies.

Trophy Note (I want to talk about it): If you complete the game and show you only have 36 conversations (there are 37), try going back and redoing this one using the second Firefly symbol (pictured below). Some people are experiencing a problem where the trophy won't pop because there are two Firefly symbols very close to each other, but the game only recognizes the second as counting towards your conversation total.

Go further forward now, and you get stopped by another downed gate. There are two conversations to have here, one about the generator, and one about the wires on the ground.

Now, crouch through the gap and into the dorm.

Artifact 60: UEC Campus Map

Grab the Artifact on the front desk here, a map of the campus.

Move through the room now, grabbing all the supplies you can find along the way. Head up the stairs and into the first room on the left. Loot this room, moving through the bathroom to the next one.

Artifact 61: Student's Journal

In the desk here (in Room 202), so grab it.

Further down the hall you run into spores. You'll have to put on your gasmask, then drop down through the floor. Oh man, there's a lot of Clickers. You need to be stealthy here, because there is also a Bloater. You can sneak your way through killing all the Clickers easily enough, and you can sneak through the rest of the way too without causing a stir.

Firefly Pendant 22: Use explosives or fire to take out the Bloater, if you want to get its treasure: a Firefly Pendant.

Move down the hall now to a door that you need to force open. Once through, head up the stairs and start looting through dorm rooms again.

Artifact 62: Newspaper Clipping

There is an Artifact on top of a mini fridge in Room 209.

Once you are done looting, take the door that leads outside. Go down the stairs and over to the generator on a cart. Push it to the side of the closed gate, and Joel will automatically plug it in. Turn it on so Ellie can raise the gate and continue forward.

Look for some blue dumpsters in this area for some supplies.

Hop on the horse and jump over the barrier here to move on to right outside the science lab.

There's no going in the front door, so loot all the medical tents outside.

Firefly Pendant 23: The farthest one away from where you entered the area from has a Firefly Pendant.

Now jump over this other barrier to keep moving forward. You see a big gaping hole in the side of the science building, so go try the gate. Rusted shut, dang. Let's find a way around now. Walk back to find a dumpster, then push it toward the rusted gate.

That worked! Let's go through the gate now. Push the dumpster over to the truck, then climb up to the truck then up further to the ledge of the building.

### Science Building

Climb into the science lab now. There are lootable Things in here. Loot all the rooms, including going all the way down the hall past the bright light to find an unlockable Shiv door.

Training Manual 10: Molotov Deployment

Behind the door are the Level 4 tools, a Training Manual and tons of supplies.

Before heading out, use the work bench to craft any upgrades you want. Head out the door behind the light in the hallway, then move around to a room with elevators.

Optional Conversation 30: Look at the clipboard on the pile of stuff here to find out you guys aren't alone in the building.

Sneak up the stairs, then go into the door that is half blocked by a table.

Artifact 63: Office Recorder

Go into the room to the left and on the bench there's an Artifact, so go listen to it.

The layout of this floor is very similar to the one below it, so go loot everything. Despite the ominous noise, there is nobody immediately up here.

Artifact 64: Fungal X-Rays

When ready, head to the hallway that is made to look like a tent. Move through here, and grab the Artifact on the counter.

When ready, open the door back here. The source of all that noise... just monkeys. Oh well.

Artifact 65: Lab Recorder

Grab the artifact on the table here and listen to it.

Firefly Pendant 24: Go to the back right corner of the room for a Firefly Pendant.

Move through to the next room and loot it. Now, open the door with the broken glass.

Artifact 66: Firefly's Recorder

In the cutscene, Joel picks it up and is automatically added to your collectibles.

Well, you aren't alone anymore! You now know where you need to go, so let's leave! There's really no good way to sneak out of here, as these guys are coming for you. Fight your way through the floor, then take the stairs back down.

Fight through here now, and go out in the lobby of the building. Open the door here and...... oh. Oh. Oh dear. That's.... wow. Yeah. You are going to have to help Ellie get you through the building, so make sure you have your hands on the controller.

# LAKESIDE RESORT

## The Hunt

Artifact 67-75: No Pun Intended, No Pun Intended: Volume Two, To Get to the Other Side!, Riley's Pendant, Sam's Robot, Walkman, Switchblade, Note from Mom, Joel & Sarah Photo

These will automatically be with Ellie. Be sure to inspect each one and flip whatever ones you can. If Ellie makes a remark or comment, that is a sign it has been registered as "collected" in the game.

Note: Ellie will not comment on the three joke books or her switchblade. Just make sure to zoom in on them and they'll still be counted as having been collected.

It's winter now! As Ellie, you will need to take down the deer with your bow. Make sure you crouch as you get closer, avoiding fallen tree branches and bushes that will make noise and spook the deer. Once you land the first hit, you will be able to follow the trail of blood to the deer's next location. Land a second arrow and it will run off to the next area. After your second arrow connects, it won't be necessary to crouch anymore. Climb over the low part in the wooden fence and continue following the blood.

You will drop down a ledge then come across a run-down building.

Comic 10: Uncertainty

If you go into the door to the left right after entering the building, you can find a Comic in a drawer.

Move forward until you are at the deer carcass to initiate a cutscene. While one of them runs back to his camp, you wait with the other. Uh oh, Clicker attack! Fight off the Infected from your position in the room.

You will be asked to help block one of the windows, so go help out. Eventually, you both will make a break for it. Follow your new partner out of the room and down the hallway. Take out the closest Clicker as your partner is barricading the door, then continue forward. Everything is going well until the walkway gives out.

Time to fight off more Infected. Sneak around taking out Clickers, or use your Bow for a ranged stealth attack. Sneak around here until you can drop below the floor. Make your way under the floor until you get to a ladder. Climb up to be reunited with your new ally. You're stuck here though, so get boosted up the side and make your way around the walkway to get to the ladder.

Firefly Pendant 25: There is a room up here that is along the back wall. Inside is a bunch of supplies and a Firefly Pendant.

Once you get to the ladder, drop it down for your pal who puts it against the other wall. Drop down, then climb the ladder up to get to the exit door.

You are now in a room and are about to be ambushed.

Optional Conversation 31: There is a body in this room. Look at it and have a conversation with David about it.

Craft as many health packs as you can and heal up, you are going to need the health. The first wave comes through the door, so throw a Molotov over there.

This will take out a few infected. The next batch will come in through the windows. It's your best bet to keep mobile and take them out with the hunting rifle. You will get a small break and a prompt to notice that a Bloater is coming in through the roof right in the middle. Toss a Molotov up there to set him ablaze immediately. Take him out fully from a distance with the hunting rifle.

Once the area is clear, follow your pal down the hallway here where Infected first came from. You will have a conversation here about Infected, and it advances to a cutscene.

**Cabin Resort**
Ride like the wind! You will have to fight off a few guys who jump onto your horse, but keep riding forward to get away from the house you are using as a base.

Eventually, you will end up back on foot. Sorry horsie. Run into the cabin ahead of you, and loot the bedrooms here. When you move into the front of the cabin, you start to hear Hunters searching for you.

Time to drop into stealth mode. Make good use of the arrows in this front room for a ranged stealth kill. Take out the guards right outside the house, then sneak out the door. There are guards all over the camp here, so watch where you go.

Firefly Pendant 26: Head over to the gazebo here to snag a collectable Firefly Pendant, then move through the cabins.

There's some loot here as well as plenty of cover. There seems to be a decent group of guys by the restrooms, so watch out for that hotspot. You eventually need to make it to the stairs at the far end of the area. Once up here, you will have to inch your way across the broken walkway to the left, then continue forward down the cliffside trail.

You drop down a bit of a drop, then crawl through a pipe. You come into a clearing, so head upstairs.

Comic 11: Negentropy

On the park bench is a collectable Comic to grab.

Now crawl through the second pipe ahead of you. It's blocked! Head back out and grab the dumpster behind the cage. Pull it out, and then head back through the pipe.

You come up on the main resort building. You can see the exit off in the distance, but don't start running for it yet. Hunters start coming out now, looking for you. Take them out, then climb on a box to drop down into the main building. You aren't alone in here, so make sure to stay as stealthy as possible.

This is a big building, but you are limited to only the downstairs. Make your way through the lobby until you get to the front entrance. Head out the door with the Exit sign above it.

Well, THAT didn't go according to plan. You're back as Joel now, so walk out of the basement you are in. Head outside and down the road. Sadly, you cannot loot any of these houses. Head forward until you stumble across some Hunters.

Take a few out, and they retreat to the back yard. Head into the back yard and into the house to find some supplies. Hop out the living room window and out to the street, and you get stopped. Watch what happens here, because it is INTENSE.

You are now back as Ellie outside in a blizzard. Run forward away from the man shooting at you. You see a door ahead of you. Blocked. Now try the door next to the gate. You're inside again. Move the cart in your way to crawl under the boards into the next room. You're now in the front of a pet store. You can hear Hunters outside, so stay behind cover.

Eventually, one enemy will enter the store. Take him out to get his gun. Make your way across the street, not down the street where everyone is heading.

Once in an alley, keep going down until you see a lot of mail trucks. Take out a few guards here, then head up the stairs. Move forward and you'll see a barrel with a fire in it. Directly to the left is a small hole you can crouch through. Head through here, and around to a pick-up truck. There may be another Hunter here, so watch out.

Continue forward through the slashed open fence. Stay along the left side of the street here until you get to an alley. There are two ways into the building here, so head in whichever way will not get you noticed by the two Hunters inside. Take them out silently, then head out the arcade's front door. There are plenty more guards outside, so make sure to move from cover to cover.

If you get spotted, run back to the gate blocking the end of the street, and hide. The Hunters cannot see very well through the snow. Eventually as you move forward down the street, you'll spot a building with a burning trash can here. Move past this to a street on the left. Follow the street now, until you get to another gate blocking the way. Jump up onto a dumpster, and then through the cracked open window.

You are now in a kitchen of some sort. It doesn't look like anyone is here or in the restaurant either. Make your way to the front door, and head outside. Ohhhh boy, our friend is back. You need to hide from him, and sneak up on him to get the keys back.

Also, as an added difficulty, he does not go down in one hit. After the first hit you land, he breaks out the machete, so now if you get hit once, you are dead. Keep after him, but without him seeing. Watch out for the smashed plates on the ground, as he will hear if you step on them. Once you land three hits, you both go down.

Artifact 76: Lake Resort Map

Joel will automatically have this in his possession at this point.

Now you are Joel again, and back outside. You come up on a gas station/garage on the right. Head inside, and hear about four Hunters coming for you. Take them out, then continue down the road outside. There's another building you can go into straight forward.

It looks like a motel. Move through the bedrooms here, until you get to the back of the motel.

Training Manual 11: Smoke Shaping

Hop out of a bathroom window and look to your left for a Shiv Door. Inside is a Training Manual and some other loot.

Now head back out. Watch out for the Hunter who is on the lookout. You can sneak into the semi trailer he is standing on without him noticing. Move past him and out the other side of the trailer. Move through the camp here until you find an alley with a burning barrel.

Continue forward, and Joel will automatically slip inside a building.

Artifact 77: Ellie's Backpack

He'll find Ellie's backpack in here that is automatically added to your possession after the cutscene.

Artifact 78: Meat Ledger

To the right of the shelf is another artifact on another shelf.

Continue forward now, being super stealthy. Move through the rest of the butcher shop and see some horrors that weren't meant to be seen. Go out the front door to see the restaurant on fire. As Ellie again, inch forward to get to the machete. Keep going after getting kicked. Be prepared to hit Triangle.

# BUS DEPOT

### Highway Exit

Optional Conversation 32: Move down the highway, talking with Ellie when you can.

Artifact 79: Family Photograph

Head into the RV to obtain a few supplies and find an Artifact.

Optional Conversation 33: Talk to Ellie about flying, then continue down the road.

Walk down the exit ramp.

Firefly Pendant 27: Right at the end on the left, behind a car near the barrier, is a Firefly Pendant.

Keep going forward down the road now. Climb from the cars up to the bus, then drop down on the other side of the wall. Head into the open building here to cut through. Head downstairs to find lots of loot.

Artifact 64: Note to Wife

Down here, on the left there is a pile of luggage and in one of the open ones is this artifact.

Look at the ladder and Joel will say something to Ellie.

Optional Conversation 34: Talk to Ellie about the ladder down here. Boost Ellie up, even though she's so reluctant.

She'll knock down the ladder, so pick it up and climb up. Ellie is super excited about something, so follow her down the hallway here. Keep going here, across an air bridge.

You see what Ellie is going on about now!

Optional Conversation 35: Walk over and pet the giraffe.

Head up the stairs and out to the roof to get a great view.


Optional Conversation 36: You can talk to Ellie up here about the giraffes.

Go into the doorway to the stairs from up here now.

The Last of Us: Part I Complete Guide

Comic 11: Precipitate

If you head into the Men's room, you can find a Comic.

Head outside and loot the medical tents.

You find the Level 5 tools out here as well as a ton of supplies.

Firefly Pendant 28: Use a brick or bottle to get a Firefly Pendant hanging on a flood light behind the large tent.

Artifact 80: Salt Lake Q.Z. Map

At the very back tent with the crafting table, you can find this artifact.

There is also a bench if you want to craft upgrades.

Optional Conversation 37: When ready, head out towards the dog barks. Ellie will come up and give you the picture of you and your daughter. (This is the last optional conversation).

Artifact 81: Joel & Sarah Photo

After the interaction with Ellie, this will be added to your backpack.

Climb through a bus, then continue down the street.

Firefly Pendant 29: You will find another Firefly Pendant behind the next bus on the road into the East Tunnel.

**Underground Tunnel**
Head down into the tunnel, and climb up over the cars in front of you. You come up on a ton of Infected. Runners, Clickers, and even three Bloaters are all ahead of you.

When you can, duck into a room on the right to find a ton of supplies. There are a few infected in the tunnel -- you can take them out quietly with the flamethrower or distract them by throwing a brick or bottle. Follow the passage and once you're back in the tunnel.

Training Manual 12: Bomb Shrapnel

Climb up the trailer truck with a red lion on it to find a Training Manual for the nail bomb.

It is possible to sneak past the infected with little or no interaction with them. If you are feeling brave, take them out. The Bloaters tend to be close to each other, which gives you a nice opportunity to take them out at the same time. If you have three nail bombs, duck behind the small fence/barricade and safely toss the bombs at them, taking them out from afar. Kill everything else that comes running your way, then continue down the tunnel to a semi. Boost Ellie up on top of the truck so that she can knock the crate down.

You get to deep water, so swim under the truck. Climb up the other side and get to the ladder to drop down for Ellie.

Comic 13: Catalysis

Climb up on the air vents and go all the way down to find a Comic.

Drop down and over to the fence to find the door blocked. Look to the far right, there is a clicker ducked down, take him out. Now boost Ellie up over the side to open it. There's a bench here to construct more upgrades. Continue forward now. On the right is a Shiv door you can open for a ton of supplies.

Once ready, duck under the rubble and you find yourself in a water filled room. Dive down here to find an open door. Take a right and go through another door to resurface. Climb up to the air vents and crawl along those now. Squeeze in between the pipes and the wall to find a wood pallet to throw down to Ellie.

Hop down yourself, and swim Ellie across the water. She'll climb up and drop down a big ladder for you. It falls off the wall, so carry it over to the gap you can't cross and lay it down.

Do this by climbing back up to that ledge you were on, pick up the ladder, drop it over by the broken walkway, climb down, then lay it across the gap. You make it to an area where the water is rushing like a river. Cross the area by jumping from bus to air vent. When you fall through the bus, mash Triangle to grab onto a bar to stop yourself.

Keep moving forward now until oh... Ellie comes to save the day, so mash Triangle again. Shit hits the fan hardcore. Dive down and swim through the door to get to Ellie. Get to her to automatically grab onto her. Keep heading forward until you get to the surface.

# THE FIREFLY LAB

## The Hospital

Oh man, that's some drama. Time to fight your way to Ellie. There are tons of ways to do this. You can shoot your way through or bypass most of the Fireflies by sneaking around them. To do this, climb through windows and duck behind counters. The cones of the flashlights give you a good idea where your enemies are looking and heading. Avoid the corridor with the two stationary guards and make a wide circle around them, picking up much needed supplies on your way.

If you eliminate the right guy, you can get an Assault rifle. Make your way to a stairway then climb up.

Artifact 82: Surgeon's Recorder

There's an Artifact right here on a counter.

Move down the hallway now, avoiding or killing guards.

FIrefly Pendant 30: There's a Shiv door over here with lots of ammo and a Firefly Pendant.

Artifact 83: Marlene's Recorder 1

From the entrance by the stairwell, to the right there is a room and in there is this recorder on a desk.

Artifact 84: Marlene's Journal

In the large quarantine tent, inside in another artifact on the table.

Now in this section, the Fireflies are actively searching for you. Try to get by the guard watching the door when he looks away and work around the right far side of the areas. Stealthily taking out a few guards, making it to the end of the corridor shouldn't be a problem with your experience up to this point of the game.

Once through the door, Joel will barricade it. Get down the hall by the pediatrics ward. When your in the hallway, open the first door to the right.

Artifact 85: Marlene's Recorder 2

In this room on the right is this artifact on the table.

Open the door at the end of the hallway and into the operating room and grab Ellie. Run now. Run through the locker room then into the elevator. Watch what happens.

# JACKSON

### Epilogue

Simply follow Joel. Once you pass the barbed wire, head to your right, away from Joel's path.

Comic 14: Singularity

There you will find a pickup truck along a rock wall. The last Artifact of the game is in the driver's seat of the truck…

## TIPS AND TRICKS

### Explore everywhere, examine everything

Survival in the apocalyptic world of The Last of Us requires scavenging for materials everywhere you can get them. Much of your success in battles will be decided by how much you've scrounged up — be it ammo for your guns, materials for making health kits, or even items for distracting enemies. Because of this, you'll want to spend as much time as possible examining every nook and cranny of each area you come across to ensure you've found all of the useful stuff that can be obtained there. Because you rarely revisit any locations, you'll usually have one opportunity to grab something — so make it count.

### Craft often and leave nothing behind

Once you've obtained enough materials to piece together a utility item like a health kit or molotov cocktail, you can open up your crafting menu to do so. It's a good rule of thumb to always keep those types of items maxed out when possible because you can only carry so many materials. If you stumble upon excess materials like alcohol or rags, use up what you have in your inventory to craft anything you don't have maxed out to ensure that you can pick up the new stuff. In other words, never leave anything behind unnecessarily.

### Use supplements wisely

You'll probably come across a lot of supplements in the form of plants and pills scattered about the post-apocalyptic world, and using these can upgrade a variety of Joel's capabilities, like Listening Mode Range, Weapon Sway, Healing Speed, and more. You won't find enough supplements in a single playthrough to upgrade every skill, so make sure you don't waste them on something that won't really make a meaningful difference. Most players are likely to get the most benefit from dumping their supplements into Maximum Health and Weapon Sway. If you manage to have enough supplements to continue upgrading skills later in the game as the difficulty increases, try tossing a point or two into Healing Speed to make sure you can get away and top off your health quicker.

### Make holster upgrades a priority

As you make your way through The Last of Us, you'll find plenty of tools and parts that can be used for upgrades at workbenches. As soon as possible, you'd do well to upgrade both of your holsters — one for pistols and one for long guns — as this will allow you to switch among up to four guns on the fly. Map your favorite weapons to those slots and ensure they're always reloaded before encounters. If you run out of ammo in one, you can still head into your backpack, scroll over to that gun, and then swap it for another one — but having four holsters ensures you don't have to do this nearly as frequently while surrounded by foes.

## Prepare before engaging

Unless you're playing it on the easiest setting, you'll find it tough to approach most fights in The Last of Us with a run-and-gun mentality. The majority of encounters in the game will require a delicate balance of stealth, melee, and conservative use of firepower. To ensure you don't have to fall back on that firepower too much or end up surrounded unexpectedly, make sure to do a bit of recon before engaging enemies. Using Joel's listening ability can give you valuable intel about where enemies are located and what kind of baddie it is, so use this as much as you can to get a feel for the flow of a room before rushing in to fight. Still, you'll find that the odds typically aren't stacked in your favor, so set up some traps and quietly take out lower-threat enemies with stealth attacks before going all out.

## Have an escape plan

As mentioned above, the odds are not going to be in your favor during most fights, and no amount of preparation can account for every single scenario. Both human and infected enemies pose a significant threat because of their ability to consistently track and run you down once you've been seen. Because of this, always try to identify areas in each location that can put distance between you and any monstrosities if things go south. You don't want to get pinned into a corner, though, so actions like vaulting through windows to the other side of a wall can often give you the short moment needed to heal or craft an item before the infected foe finds a path to you.

## Always keep shivs around

Shivs are one of your most precious resources in The Last of Us. If you're overrun by enemies and find yourself grabbed by an always-terrifying Clicker, a shiv acts as a defensive item that can be used to instantly kill the enemy and let you escape an otherwise guaranteed death. Additionally, shivs can be used to open a variety of locked doors that stand between you and rooms filled to the brim with helpful resources. Sometimes you'll even find materials needed to craft more shivs inside, making it well worth your while to use one to access the room. All of that said, don't bother wasting those same materials to upgrade melee weapons, as crafting more shivs will almost always be more beneficial.

### Pick up your fired arrows

The bow, which is obtained fairly early in the game, is among the deadliest and most efficient parts of Joel's kit. Its ability to kill enemies with a single arrow at range while keeping you safe in stealth is extremely helpful in large-scale encounters, and with some upgrades to its draw speed, it can even be an impressive weapon during intense shootouts. Best of all, though, is that each arrow has a chance of not breaking upon hitting an enemy, meaning you'll sometimes have an opportunity to retrieve them from dead bodies. After you've downed an enemy, keep an eye out for shiny arrows protruding from their corpses and make sure not to leave any behind.

### Save frequently

The Last of Us has a liberal autosave feature, so you typically won't have to worry about replaying massive segments of the game after dying. However, it's worth noting that you can also perform manual saves to ensure that you can roll back some of your decisions. If you've just survived an intense showdown by the skin of your teeth, you may be disappointed at how much ammo or resources it took to achieve success. There's nothing wrong with accepting the outcome of that hard-fought victory and pushing forward, but there's also no shame in reverting to a save just before the battle to give it another go in hopes of walking away in better shape — especially on higher difficulties where every bullet and material is precious. Do what's best for you.

# ABOUT THE AUTHOR

I When I finding new tricks, tips, and strategies to beat each other, they came up with a brilliant idea. Let's take these hours of gaming expertise, and share these skills with like mind people. At that moment, the The Last of Us: Part I Complete Guide were born. With more exciting gaming books being developed in the Lab as we speak. I am creating a buzz in the gaming guide publishing world, with a ground swell of followers, anxiously awaiting my new releases.

Made in United States
North Haven, CT
13 December 2023